FARNHAM PORTRAIT

BASED ON THE FARNHAM HERALD SERIES 'MICHAEL BLOWER'S ENVIRONMENTAL VIEWPOINT'

Drawings by Michael Blower : Words by Susan Farrow

with a foreword by **NIGEL TEMPLE,** M.Litt., Ph.D., A.T.D., R.W.A.
Author of 'Farnham Buildings and People'

Ashgate Editions

1989
Ashgate editions
Gower House, Croft Road, Aldershot, Hampshire GU11 3HR

ISBN 0 85967 838 5

Book design by Susan Farrow
Location plans drawn by Matthew Lake

Printed and bound in England by
Signland Limited, The Trading Estate, Farnham, Surrey GU9 9NN

CONTENTS

LIST OF DRAWINGS

(eight reproduced in full colour)

Farnham street scenes

Cover : High Mill

FOREWORD by Nigel Temple, M.Litt, Ph.D, ATD, RWA

The talents of Susan Farrow and Michael Blower have combined to produce more than one hundred and thirty 'Environmental Viewpoint' articles for the *Farnham Herald*. This new book draws from and expands on that considerable achievement.

Some subjects are familiar to us all. We might even take them for granted, considering them to be secure features of the Farnham scene for all foreseeable time. This is a dangerous state of mind. But the authors select also less obvious subjects — barns, neglected gardens, alleyways — which contribute so much to the urban fabric, yet can disappear almost overnight.

Perhaps the most poignant drawings are those capturing that delicate balance between transient visual coherence and pending irreversible change. Herein lies a dilemma for those visually alert who have a civic conscience.

Susan Farrow and Michael Blower not only chronicle change in Farnham, but also inform, discuss, explain, warn, and educate with exceptional dedication. Simultaneously they entertain.

19 October 1989

THE AUTHORS

MICHAEL BLOWER, F.R.I.B.A., A.A.Dipl., F.R.S.A., is an architect with a special interest in conservation, with his own practice in Farnham. He was a County Councillor from 1983-1985, Chairman of the Farnham Society from 1986-1989, and Secretary to the Farnham (Buildings Preservation) Trust Ltd from 1973-1988. He was a member of the working group which in the early 1970s made recommendations for the listing of historic buildings in Farnham. He is now Vice-Chairman of the Farnham (Buildings Preservation) Trust Ltd and a Vice-President of the Farnham Society.

SUSAN FARROW came to Farnham in 1979. She became Secretary of the Farnham Society in 1984, and Secretary to the Farnham (Buildings Preservation) Trust Ltd in 1988.

The authors have collaborated to produce the weekly *Farnham Herald* series 'Michael Blower's Environmental Viewpoint' since February 1987. By November 1989, when this book was published, 138 articles had appeared in the series, which was still continuing. The first 16 articles were published in book form in 1988 under the title 'Farnham — Moments in View'.

INTRODUCTION

This book is based on a series of articles from the *Farnham Herald* series 'Environmental Viewpoint' which started in February 1987. Week by week since that time, the series has focussed on a succession of Farnham buildings and street scenes, recording each one as it appeared at the time when the article was written. In choosing the subjects, we have ranged between the old and the new, the urban and the rural, the great and the small, and the famous and the little-known, gradually building up a composite picture of the town in the late 1980s.

FARNHAM PORTRAIT takes a selection of the 130 articles which appeared over 2½ years, and groups them to present three particular aspects of the town: 'Green Farnham — mills, riverside and farms'; 'Farnham houses'; and 'Farnham street scenes'. The subjects are illustrated with 73 of Michael Blower's drawings, accompanied by a description in words including the historical and architectural background.

Each subject is precisely located by its own small street plan, so that as well as being a portrait, the book will, we hope, function as a guide for people who enjoy exploring the less well-known corners of the town.

Some aspects of Farnham, such as its network of old yards and lanes, have not been included in this book, although many of the articles have described them. We hope to publish these later.

We owe a great debt to Nigel Temple, whose scholarly research, contained in his book 'Farnham Buildings and People', has been our constant reference and indispensable aid. In a small way, we feel that we are following in his august footsteps in producing this book, and we are immensely gratified that he has contributed its Foreword.

We must also thank Robin Radley, editor of the *Farnham Herald*, for keeping a space in his busy newspaper every week for the 'Environmental Viewpoint' articles, and for continuing to support the project so enthusiastically, and we gratefully acknowledge the skilled and friendly assistance provided by Mike Smith of Signland, in printing the book.

The *Farnham Herald* series on which the book is based was written as the environmental viewpoint of two people who love Farnham and who have a deep concern for its future. That same thread runs through the book.

Susan Farrow
14 October 1989

THE MILL HOUSE. HATCH MILL.

2

Michael Blower. 12 March 1989.

GREEN FARNHAM~ MILLS, RIVERSIDE & FARMS

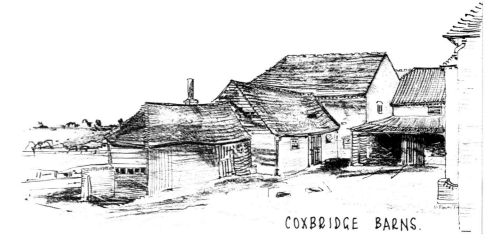

COXBRIDGE BARNS.

If you pass through the churchyard, a passage way at the opposite corner takes you right out into the church meadow, by the winding river. Across this rich pasture land runs a footpath leading to a delicious watermill, standing close up against the hill to the south of the town, where it rises with precipitous suddenness almost from the margin of the rushing stream.

Home Handbook for Farnham
by Major Gordon Home (1900)

These words written about Farnham in 1900 are still almost as true today as they were then. The 'delicious watermill' (Weydon Mill) has disappeared, but in spite of the modern pressure for development in the remaining open spaces in the town, the riverside has survived as a corridor of green running right through the centre. It is a forgotten place seen by few people other than walkers and the children who play there.

The meadows which used to be cut for hay have now grown wild, and they have become a natural sanctuary for wild life, existing peacefully a few hundred yards away from the busy shopping streets and car parks. The River Wey passes by self-effacingly, seen only where it slides silently past the Maltings, under Longbridge, through Gostrey Meadow and under South Street to Borelli Walk. In the modern town, the focus has shifted away from the waterside.

Yet Farnham is essentially a river town. It has always been dominated by the fact that it grew up in the narrow bottom of a small sheltered valley, around the wide shallow river crossing which is now Longbridge. The Saxon name 'Fearnhamme' derives from words meaning 'fern growing in heathland, and useful water meadows' and this description conjures up a picture of a gentle and hospitable place.

Until the 19th century, the people of Farnham depended on their river to make their lives possible. It gave them a sheltered position below the geological 'Farnham Terraces' which it had gradually cut out in prehistoric times; it gave them flat meadows and fertile soil for their crops; it gave them watermills, ponds where swans could be kept, and fish hatcheries; and it also gave them gravel, sand and clay which supported local industries.

In spite of all the other factors which have brought prosperity to Farnham over the centuries — the presence of the lordly Bishops of Winchester in their Castle, the great wheat market, and the hop industry — it is the river and the town's valley situation which have given it its enduringly and endearingly rural character.

One of Farnham's most potent characteristics is the fact that the centre is so small, with so much green around it. Since the railway came in 1840 there has been a great deal of expansion and new building, but the town's compact central street plan — a consequence of the narrow valley situation — has kept development away from the open spaces.

Farnham Park and the farm fields to the north and west of the town spread a green backcloth behind the mellow buildings in the valley. There is a working farm in West Street, less than a mile from the foot of Castle Street. Meadows edge the river all the way through the town and along the bypass. Many of the old mills have survived, with 17th and 18th century buildings. Under the thin veneer of modern commercial life, Farnham remains what it has been for so long, a small country town.

In the Domesday Book of 1086, the Hundred, Manor and Parish of Farnham was credited with six watermills, among 5000 in the country as a whole. The Farnham mills were not named and they cannot be identified with any certainty, but there have been mills on the River Wey since Saxon times, possibly even since the Romans, and the list is likely to have included Willey Mill, Bourne Mill, High Mill, Elstead Mill, Weydon Mill and Hatch Mill or Rock Mill. There are still buildings on all these sites except Weydon Mill, which was demolished in 1919 because of its dilapidated condition despite local protests, and Rock Mill, of which only vestiges remain, hidden in undergrowth beside Moor Park Lane.

Local mills have had many different names. Weydon Mill in particular has been named in a variety of ways in maps and documents, as Meads Mill, Farnham Mill, Sluice Mill, Hangars Mill, West Mill and La Medmulle. Hatch Mill is also East Mill and Bishops Mill, and after different millers, Piggott's, Pisley's and Darvill's Mill (hence Darvills Lane).

Bourne Mill has the oldest buildings, dating back to the 17th century while Willey Mill, High Mill and Hatch Mill are 18th century. All are Grade II listed buildings. The Bourne Mill now has an incongruous setting beside Guildford Road near the Shepherd and Flock roundabout, separated from its village by the circling traffic.

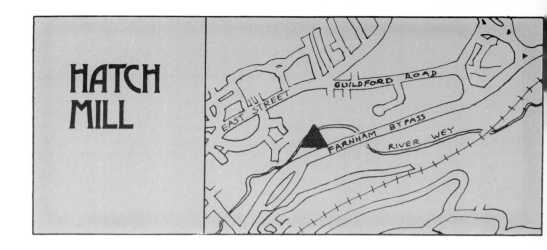

HATCH MILL

Hatch Mill is one of four old mills on the eastern side of the town, the others being Bourne Mill, High Mill and Rock Mill. Three of the four survive today, Rock Mill having vanished many years ago.

Hatch Mill's setting changed radically when the eastern section of the Farnham Bypass was built in the late 1930s. Before that, it stood among quiet meadows approached only by Darvills Lane from Hickley's Corner, and it is said that an occupant used to shoot pheasants (unofficially) from his bedroom window in the mill house across what is now a dual-carriageway.

Most of Darvills Lane disappeared when the new A31 road was built, and Hatch Mill is now isolated, a little below the level of the road and dominated by the traffic which speeds past. The main part of the building is used as the Redgrave Theatre rehearsal studios and wardrobe store, but the mill house is still lived in, although it is close to the bypass 5 feet above, and separated from it only by some trees and shrubs.

Hatch Mill (the word 'hatch' is Saxon, meaning gate) ceased to function as a mill in 1901 when it became Hatch Mill Laundry. In 1938, then called Farnham Sanitary Laundry, it was seriously affected by the plans for the new bypass when Surrey County Council as the highway authority proposed the compulsory purchase of 3½ of the laundry's 5 acres. As it was at first planned, the new road would have cut across a corner of the mill house, but fortunately it was agreed instead that the line would run a little to the south, leaving the building intact.

The laundry's directors at the time wrote graphically in a letter to the County Council about the effect the road would have on the mill house. They foresaw "the reduction in value of the Dwelling House which will take place owing to the close proximity of the new road, the traffic from which will produce much noise and dust, and further the level of the road being some 5 feet above the ground floor of the main sitting rooms, the annoyance of fast traffic continually whizzing past above the eye level will be very marked. At present the house and laundry are surrounded by pasture and the house enjoys a privacy which will be entirely lost."

These words came true to an extent which in 1938 could hardly have been envisaged, with the volume of traffic using the bypass in the 1980s.

Before the bypass, the mill stood on a little island with the river on one side, and on the other, a stream which passed under the building. When the road was constructed, the mill stream was filled in, together with the milltail, sluice and pond. Two wells were put in to provide a water supply for the laundry, and the directors succeeded in getting compensation of just under £8,500 which included the purchase of land at £300 an acre, and the cost of putting up new buildings.

Today, in spite of the traffic roaring past, the mill house looks serene and peaceful. It is a pretty 18th century building, with carefully laid red bricks under a slate roof, small-paned sash windows, and climbing plants on the walls. The porch over the front door is simple and elegant, with fluted white pilasters and a semi-circular fanlight.

Apart from the bypass, the surroundings of Hatch Mill are still quite rural. The river passes to the north of the mill buildings between weed-grown banks and under trailing willows, and the new Abbeyfield House and Riverside Court on the opposite side impinge very little.

After passing Hatch Mill, the river turns southwards and dives under the bypass, emerging in deep water meadows to run beside the lane leading to Snayleslynch Farm and the Kilns. Snayleslynch is believed to be the oldest settlement in the area, but although the present buildings, with their river frontage, look ancient, they are not the oldest in the town. From Snayleslynch the path continues through fields for a short distance to High Mill.

DOORCASE AT HATCH MILL HOUSE.

HIGH MILL.

Michael Blower

HIGH MILL

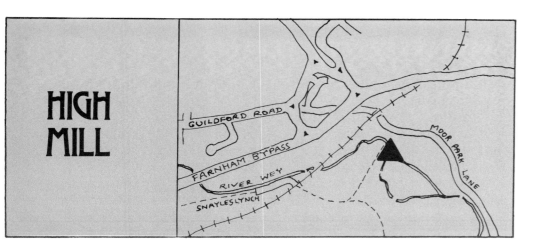

High Mill is nowhere near any modern traffic. It can be reached by the footpath from Snayleslynch, but to get to it by car one must drive on to the Shepherd and Flock roundabout, pass through the old Bourne Mill village, and go along Moor Park Lane under, first, the concrete tunnel carrying the bypass, and then the brick railway bridge.

Then the lane is shadowed on one side by the vestiges of an old wall all overgrown and broken by mysterious hollows, said to be the remains of the medieval Rock Mill. There used to be a waterfall here, but it dried up many years ago.

High Mill is now a private house. Seen from Moor Park Lane, it lies across a meadow, its red brick glowing in the sun, beside the river among willow trees. The public footpath passes in front of it, going back via Snayleslynch and Darvills Lane to Hickley's Corner and the town.

In spite of its name, High Mill does not stand on high ground. The name comes from the old English word 'haeg' meaning 'enclosure', and the mill was named as 'la hyghe' in 1258 and as 'Hyde Mill' in 1823.

The 17th century mill machinery is still there, made of wood — a rare survival of millwork of the time. The water wheel is made of iron with wooden floats. The mill is three storeys high, with the millstones on the first floor and above, deep holds for grain. In *The Mill on the Floss,* George Eliot wrote that the second floor was the part of the mill Maggie Tulliver liked best — the corn-hatch, where she could sit on the heaps of grain.

Both the mill house and the mill itself, with its historic machinery, are Grade II listed buildings. They are shown side by side in the drawing, seen from the edge of the mill pond through a veil of overhanging willows. The setting is idyllic in summer, with long willow fronds trailing over shallow brown water in which trout can be seen, the shimmer of blue-green dragonflies hovering over the weed beds, and the occasional blue flash of a passing kingfisher.

The mill has the substantial form which is typical of such buildings, and it has been said that mills in Farnham have similarities. High Mill bears some constructional resemblance to a model of Weydon Mill which is in Farnham Museum, and to pictures and drawings of the now vanished building.

The lower storey is of brick, and the two upper storeys of dark boarding. The tiled roof is mansarded with a change of angle one-third of the way down, and hipped back at the gables at the intersection of the two slopes. The house is also of brick at ground floor level, with tile-hanging above, sashed windows and white-painted woodwork. In the barn to the left of the mill, as seen in the drawing, there is a dovecote around which white doves flutter and murmur.

The scene is truly delightful.

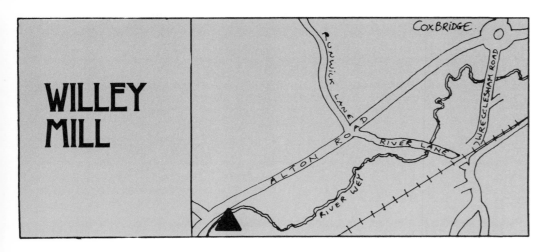

WILLEY MILL

Here is a river with fine meadows on each side of it, and with rising grounds on each outside of the meadows, those grounds having some hop-gardens and some pretty woods.

William Cobbett
Rural Rides, 1825

These words describe the setting of Willey Mill. Writing in 1825, William Cobbett said that the valley between Farnham and Alton had been called "the finest 10 miles in England" and the scene has changed little since. The railway runs along rising ground to the south of the river, but it is hidden by trees. The old turnpike road has become a modern dual carriageway, and the hop-gardens have gone, but otherwise Cobbett would recognise it. The road stretches westward into Hampshire, following the valley with its flat water meadows where cattle graze, and flocks of wild geese congregate in winter. The slow-running River Wey meanders quietly over its deep-cut bed, its smooth surface reflecting silvery-leafed willows.

In winter, the river almost always rises above its banks to flood the meadows with shallow water which stands for weeks at a time, attracting great numbers of sea birds and waders (and attendant bird watchers).

The valley sides enclose the view, but because the hills are low the light sweeps in from east and west painting patterns of colour and shadow where grassy slopes meet dark woods. There are spectacular sunsets, especially in winter when the sun slants from the horizon. At all seasons and in all weathers, this gentle stretch of countryside is a place which lifts the spirit.

Willey Mill is about a mile from the Coxbridge roundabout at a point where the river's meanders have taken it close to the road, and the village of Wrecclesham shows as rooftops dotted about among the trees on the southern hill. The name of the mill belongs to the district, coming from the Saxon 'wae-leage' which means 'shrine'. A public footpath runs through the mill grounds and crosses the river meadows to Wrecclesham, and the drawing shows the 18th century mill house surrounded by trees, with a small humped bridge over the stream in front.

Cobbett's valley, however, is likely to change out of recognition by the end of the century. Under the fields and woods lie vast deposits of sand, and there is already a gargantuan pit between the railway and Wrecclesham, its moon landscape busy with machinery and conveyor belts, and its great gaping mouth fed by a stream of lorries dumping refuse, like birds trying to satisfy the demands of some monstrous cuckoo in the nest.

The land between the river and the railway was acquired by a sand extraction company in the 1980s and prospect areas for new mineral working were identified in the fields between the railway and the Alton Road, following the line of the river to within a few yards of the mill. Even the fact that this stretch of countryside is designated in the Surrey Structure Plan as an Area of Great Landscape Value, and is subject to policies restricting development, is apparently not enough to prevent this disastrous threatened industrialisation of the valley.

Through a 15 or 20-year cycle, the land from which the sand has been taken will be refilled with rubbish, covered with a layer of topsoil, and restored to grazing land, but experience in the pit on the other side of the railway line has shown that the backfilling

WILLEY MILL HOUSE.

Michael Blower
Sept '87

9

causes many problems, such as the generation of methane gas from waste materials.

There is also a plan for a rail depot for aggregates, with a permanent industrial complex at the side of the existing pit, which will inevitably mean that heavy lorries will be coming and going from the A31, with noise and dust.

The value of the valley to Farnham as a piece of undisturbed countryside lies not solely in its intrinsic landscape quality but also in its situation so close to the town, forming part of its green frame. When final decisions are taken about new sandpits, commerce and conservation will be put in the scales and weighed against each other. If the scales come down in favour of commerce, and little weight is attached to conservation, it will be a sad day for Farnham.

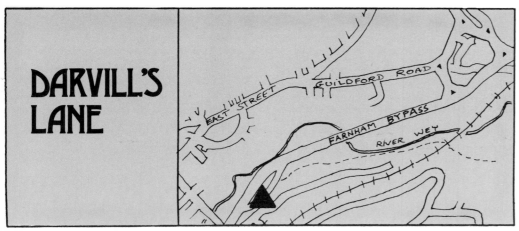

Before the eastern section of the Farnham Bypass was built in the late 1930s, Darvills Lane ran from the town at Hickley's Corner, and across open meadows to Hatch Mill. It is named after a miller. The bypass cut a swathe across the area, and swallowed Darvills Lane almost completely, leaving only a small loop off the southern side of the dual carriageway. The lane then runs parallel with the main road, to Snayleslynch Farm.

The points where Darvills Lane meets the bypass are unsign-posted and easy to miss in the fast-moving stream of traffic, so perhaps it is not surprising that few people know it is there. But for those who turn away from the traffic to explore this secretive place, a treat lies in store.

Enclosed by the loop of the lane are the Victorian buildings which used to be the property of the Mid-Southern Water Board. The first building is a dwelling house, a little dilapidated and with an ugly extension at the back, but still possessing many pretty touches of architectural detail which make it a pleasure to look at. In the morning sun, it glows with colour from the roof tiles and warm-toned bricks, which are set off by decorative courses of yellow bricks.

The roof has bands of ornamental tiles which produce an attractively varied textural effect, and it is crowned by a line of ridge tiles with upstanding finials at each end. The chimneys are of unusual design, widening at the top with relief patterning in brick.

Beyond this house are three more attractive buildings of a small-scale industrial type, with gracefully flaring roof lines and tall arched windows with ornamental iron glazing bars, built in red brick with tiled roofs and decorative finials. When the drawing was done in late 1988, the whole site was empty and neglected, the buildings standing forlornly around an open yard, with ivy growing thickly over the roof and along a broken gutter.

The lane leading to Snayleslynch runs behind the Water Board buildings, at a higher level halfway up the steep bank on top of which are the gardens and houses of Bridgefield. It is over-shadowed by the bank and arched over by dark holly trees. Then it drops down to meet the river, which appears from a tunnel under the bypass to run alongside, sometimes slow-moving, smooth and shining, and sometimes bubbling cheerfully over stones. Untended willow trees make linear patterns over the water, horizontal and vertical, and the banks are overgrown with nettles. It is extraordinary to find such a natural strip of land so

GROUP OF WATER BOARD BUILDINGS AT DARVILLS LANE.

Michael Blower 24 Nov 88

close to the bypass, in sight of the Guildford Road Industrial Estate.

Darvills Lane is recognised in the Waverley Local Plan and given the special status of an Area of Strategic Visual Importance. This is a bureaucratic way of saying that it is a pretty little piece of natural open land which is particularly important because it is close to the built-up area, and the Plan policy says that it should not be developed. Permission was granted in 1987 for a low-key office development using the old Water Board buildings, which would not cause much disturbance to the peaceful setting of the lane. But in 1989, a public inquiry into a proposal for a service station for motorists with shop, restaurant nd business facilities on the water board site caused a great public outcry. People in Farnham love and value their quiet open spaces, and they turned out in large numbers to attend the Inquiry, and to try to defend Darvills Lane from such a radical change.

Sentiment apart, the service station proposal represents a potential turning point in planning terms, because if the policy covering Darvills Lane is not upheld, a precedent is set which affects other areas in the same category, such as the fields behind Beavers Road in the town, and the Manley Bridge Valley.

Open space must be valued for its own sake. To make the assumption, as some do, that there will always be development of a kind in such an area is to jeopardise an irreplaceable asset.

THE PUMP HOUSE

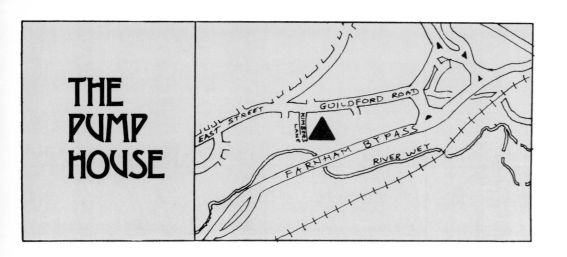

A riverside walk runs eastwards from South Street towards the Shepherd and Flock roundabout, parallel to the bypass. Where the path meets the end of Kimbers Lane, there is a delightful example of Victorian industrial architecture — the Pump House.

This building, unmarked on modern maps and little known, in fact represents the beginning of a new era in Farnham because it was the pumping station for the first low-level piped sewer to be brought into use in the town, inaugurated in 1887.

The Farnham Water Company, formed in 1837, spent a number of years looking for a suitable site for the sewage pumping station — not easy, because people feared that it would be a smelly neighbour. Eventually the company settled on half an acre of land owned by William Kimber in Guildford Road.

The architect Thomas Wonnacott, known in the late 19th century for his non-conformist churches and chapels in the town, may have been associated with the setting up of the pumping station, but this is uncertain. Whoever designed the Pump House, it is an interesting building, low and compact but with steeply pitched roofs displaying many contrasting planes and angles. The outlines of the roof slopes are dramatically defined with red hip tiles, and small ventilators are let into the roof all around the building, louvred and with white-painted carved bargeboards.

The segments of the building are drawn together by a lantern at the top, surmounted by a weather vane.

The building's most notable feature is the repeated arches on all its sides, made of hard Staffordshire blue bricks alternating with red 'rubbers' (rubbed bricks). Contrasted with the yellow bricks of the main structure, the effect is very striking.

In 1982, the Pump House was derelict. It had been used for a time as storage space by a model railway club, but it was then just a shell and virtually uninhabitable, its only water supply coming from an outside tap.

Today, the building is transformed. It was taken over by Waverley Training Services, and was completely renovated by trainees working under expert supervision. It is now a centre for practical training for young people between the ages of 16 and 20 (some of them are disabled). They learn horticulture, building work of all kinds, retailing, clerical work and computers. As well as making the Pump House the bright friendly place it is today, they have also made a garden and a patio, and they have two allotments.

The fact that the trainees and staff have done the building up themselves gives them a strong sense of personal involvement and pride which is good for the people and good for the building.

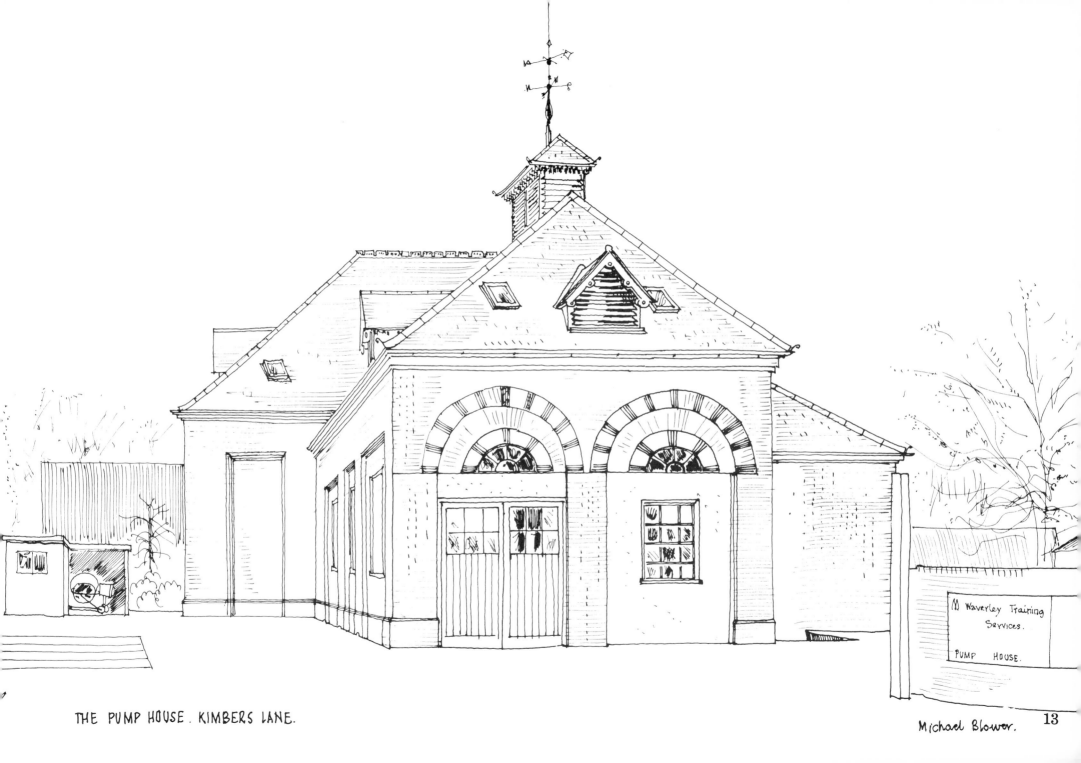

THE PUMP HOUSE. KIMBERS LANE.

Michael Blower.

13

GOSTREY MEADOW

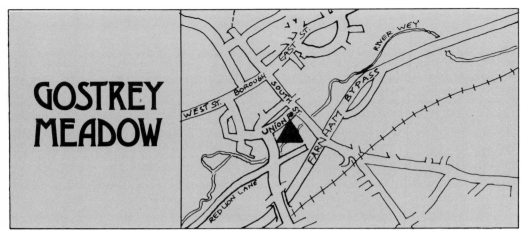

Gostrey Meadow today is a popular place with children's swings, a slide and a sandpit, enclosed by trees and shrubs, the river and its banks forming a natural focus. At the South Street end there is a little hump-backed foot bridge and a small garden surrounding the War Memorial.

Bounded by Longbridge, Union Road and South Street, with the river on its fourth side, Gostrey Meadow imparts to this area a sense of space whose value cannot be over-estimated. In the crowded town of the 1980s, Farnham people should be very thankful that the councillors in 1910 got their priorities right.

Public gardens and formally laid out parks are not Farnham's style. In a town with 300 acres of natural parkland including a cricket field and a golf course, and river meadows running right through the centre, there is plenty of open space, and when Gostrey Meadow was proposed in 1908 as a public recreation ground, some people felt it was superfluous.

At the time, Gostrey Meadow was a muddy field mainly used as a place to deposit road sweepings, and it flooded every winter. Visitors arriving at the railway station were whisked in covered wagons straight to the Bush Hotel so that they would not see this deplorably untidy sight which let down the town's new image as a tourist attraction. The town elders had already decided to plant trees in South Street to hide the mess.

Money was raised to turn this eyesore into an attractive recreation ground, and in 1910 the work was well under way, with gifts from well-wishers. A drinking fountain placed near the Union Road entrance was designed by the architect Harold Falkner, and in 1912 C.E. Borelli marked his retirement as Chairman of the Council by presenting a shelter beside the bowling green.

DRINKING FOUNTAIN IN GOSTREY MEADOW, WITH CHURCH HOUSE BEHIND.

FOOTBRIDGE IN GOSTREY MEADOW. WITH THE MALTINGS, POLICE STATION, AND PARISH CHURCH IN THE BACKGROUND.

THE FARNHAM MALTINGS

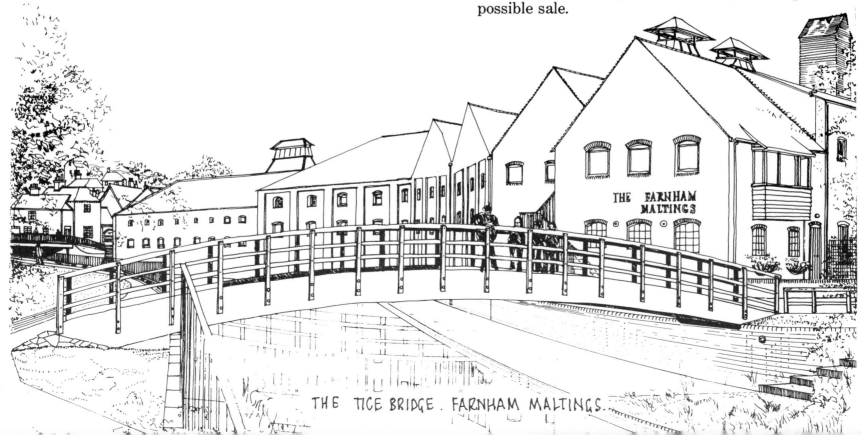

No description of the Farnham riverside would be complete without mention of the Maltings. Its substantial form dominates the west side of Longbridge, and the long outline of its buildings overshadows the river. With its shallow roof slopes and sharp gable ends, this relic of the prosperous brewing industry marches beside the river in sections, angled like an old-fashioned screen. Its high brick walls, in subtly changing shades of red above a grey plinth, are pierced by many small windows, typical of this sort of working building.

The recent history of the Farnham Maltings is legendary. In 1969, the turn-of-the-century buildings were scheduled for demolition and replacement with a development of maisonettes. A packed public meeting of Farnham people decided that this could not be allowed to happen, and incredibly, the sum of £30,000 was raised in the short period offered by Courage Brewery for a possible sale.

THE TICE BRIDGE. FARNHAM MALTINGS.

THE MALTINGS, FROM RED LION LANE

The Maltings was bought, and since that time the straggle of neglected and derelict riverside buildings has gradually been transformed into the thriving independent community and arts centre of today, the pride of Farnham and the focus for most of the activities which go on in this exceptionally lively and creative town.

West of the Maltings lies the wildest part of the river meadows. To appreciate it, one has only to pause for a while on the Tice Bridge, the little humped footbridge which was placed beside the Maltings in memory of Alan Perrett Tice, who died in 1975.

From this point the river curves away gently to the west. Seen on a cloudy autumn morning the view is clothed in sombre tints of grey, green and sepia, with the sky dark above fields browned by frost. The church tower stands out white in the background, and willow, sycamore and alder edge the river, separating it from the car park in the Wagon Yard. In the distance an ivy-grown willow tree shows in silhouette, leaning over the stream, and it is startling thus to encounter the detached, self-contained quality of the countryside in winter, just behind the busy streets.

Footpaths run through these deserted meadows, but you cannot reach them from the Maltings. To get to them, you have to go to the churchyard, where a path slips between the walls in the south-west corner. Maybe some day there will be a footpath all along the river, so that more people will be able to enjoy this lonely landscape, so astonishingly close to the centre of the town.

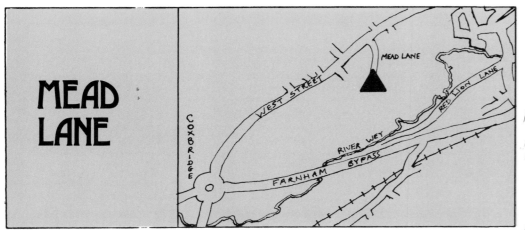

MEAD LANE

There are very few points of public access to the river meadows from West Street. One is from the churchyard, and the other is from Mead Lane, or from Babbs Mead which runs between Crosby's factory and the Memorial Hall to join Mead Lane at its foot.

None of these points is easy to find unless you are certain of your way and a newcomer exploring Mead Lane is easily put off by the barrier of the factory buildings and yards. The footpath runs between high wire fences lined with incongruous-looking evergreen trees which partly screen buildings of corrugated green metal like aircraft hangars. The fences are hung with forbidding warning signs, and there is little to encourage a casual walker hoping to find more attractive scenery.

The reward for persistence comes eventually in the form of a rusted white-painted metal gate, opening on to a picturesque view with a clear track ahead leading across the meadows to a bridge over the river, with the cottages of Red Lion Lane on the other side. For centuries there was a watermill here beside the bridge, an important feature of life in the town. This was Weydon Mill, described as it was in 1900 in the quotation at the beginning of this chapter (p.3).

MEAD LANE.

Michael Blower 7 Sept 88

THE RIVER MEADOWS, LOOKING TOWARDS RED LION LANE.

This mill was part of the considerable estate owned by the Vernon family of West Street, and in the 18th century it had three or possibly even four pairs of grinding stones under its roof. In 1919 the building was declared to be unsafe, and despite attempts to save it, was demolished. The miller's house stood until the late 1950s, but it had by then been empty for some time and was in a ruinous condition. The only visible signs of the old mill now are the watercourse and the walls between which the big wheel was located.

Mead Lane between West Street and the factory area is very attractive. It slopes steeply down towards the river, with pretty cottages and houses standing at the road's edge, to a point beside the football ground where there is a small community of chalkstone and flint buildings. In the 18th century there were two tanyards here, but in the 19th century hops took over and the buildings became drying kilns. Tanyard Kiln is long gone, but

Hart Kiln is still there, a long chalkstone building with a slate roof, stretching eastwards towards the church. Facing it is a row of cottages with red-tiled roofs and chalkstone walls, with small fenced gardens shaded by apple trees, and the church tower looking over the rooftops.

The Memorial Sports Ground, now the home of Farnham Town Football Club, was known in the 19th century as Sampson's Meadow, and Sampson's Almshouses, now demolished, stood where the car park is now. Sampson Sampson, a maltster whose name is painted on the side of a house in Bridge Square, lived at 40 West Street.

There is a strong sense of history in the little enclave at the foot of Mead Lane, in spite of the forbidding presence of Crosby's. The juxtaposition of the two provides a graphic illustration of the difference between local industries in the 18th and 19th centuries, and a modern one.

COXBRIDGE FARM

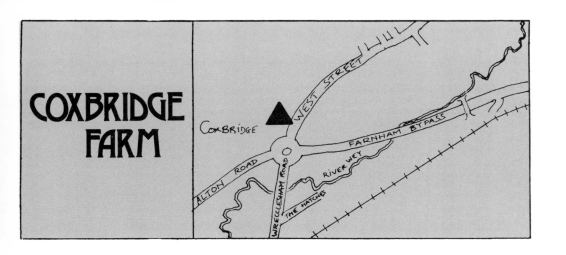

How many towns with a population between 30 and 40 thousand can boast a working farm less than a mile from the centre? Farnham can, and the sight of a herd of black and white cows grazing in fields alongside a modern traffic roundabout is a striking manifestation of the interface between two worlds.

The farm fields encircle the roundabout, and extend northwards to the edge of Crondall Lane in 150 acres of grazing land with softly undulating and sloping meadows, and a little stream whose shingle banks are lined with willows, once cut for basket-making. The stream is fed by springs beside Crondall Lane, which in turn have their origin in water running off the high chalk land at Old Park, and it is clearly shown on old maps of the area, running down to join the river Wey in the valley. Trout are still found in it.

Past the factory and a few hundred yards further out along West Street, built-up Farnham comes to an abrupt end. After the Chantrys estate and the cemetery, farm fields take over and just before the roundabout which joins West Street and Wrecclesham Road with the A31, the group of buildings comprising Coxbridge Farm stands on the north side of the road. Coxbridge is still a working farm, with a prize-winning herd of Friesian cows.

COXBRIDGE FARM, FROM THE ROAD.

Michael Blower Apl.

20

COXBRIDGE FARM, FROM THE EAST.

The farmhouse buildings go back a long way. The group consists of a three-bay 16th century building whose timber framing shows on the east-facing wall; a large 18th century addition on its west side; and an attached 18th century cottage on the road front. 18th century barns in autumn-shaded brick and tile stand beside the road, and beyond are the more modern buildings of Bushy Reeds Farm, now incorporated as part of Coxbridge.

The farm has been run since 1970 by the Kenward family, as tenants of the owners, Surrey County Council. It was once a hop farm, and old field names are recorded on the tithe map of 1840 — Mawfield, beside West Street; Mortons Field; Breakneck Hill Piece; Lone Barn Platt; Hook Edge; Dippenhall Stone Pond Piece; Randalls; Smith Close; Shortbishops; and Turnpike Field beside the Alton road where a toll cottage must have stood.

Inside, the farmhouse is a classic of its kind, with a huge kitchen and a panelled parlour. The Georgian staircase has turned balusters, and behind it is a finely-shaped 'sun-ray' cupboard. The rooms in the 16th century part of the house are low-ceilinged, and it has been suggested that originally there was a hearth in the middle of the old main room, with a chimney added at the back later.

Seen from the road, Coxbridge Farm belies its age. The fronts of the farmhouse and cottage have been plastered and have a Victorian appearance. There is little hint of its long history, or the sense of antiquity which pervades the old house, or the peace of the walled garden. Few of the people who pass it every day know it for what it is, a hidden treasure.

MANLEY BRIDGE FARM

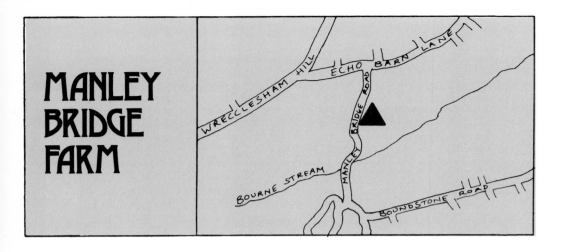

The small strip of countryside bordering Manley Bridge Road, a green margin between Wrecclesham and Rowledge, is a delight. This unspoiled valley has steeply sloping meadows which climb up on each side of the Bourne stream, here newly risen in Alice Holt and running to meet the bigger river in Moor Park. On its way the stream passes under Fullers Road in Holt Pound, under Manley Bridge, and goes on through Upper, Middle and Lower Bourne in its own small valley parallel to that of the Wey.

At Manley Bridge, the stream's course is marked by clumps of willow, ash and hawthorn, and its shallow water bubbles over big stones between banks which in summer are deep in meadowsweet and hemlock, blackberry and wild rose.

The fields on each side of the road belong to Manley Bridge Farm, whose cluster of weather-beaten barns stands on a bend halfway up the hill on the Wrecclesham side. The farm dates back 200 years, and has been owned for almost all of this time by the Turner family, who still live there.

The history of the original landholding, however, goes back much further, to 1552 when the Bishop of Winchester's records mention a close of "purpresture" land (i.e. an enclosure out of waste land) containing two acres and called Manley Reed. The holding was built up gradually over succeeding years, and became a farm in its own right in 1790.

A plan of the farm in 1840 shows it in the ownership of Thomas Lickfold Turner, with hopfields bordering the stream, and pasture land reaching up to what is now called Echo Barn Lane, which was then known as Pipers Lane going westwards, and Stickhams Lane going eastwards. A few years later, in the hands of Thomas Turner's second son James, the farm expanded and grew to extend from Holt Pound to Sandrock Hill Road. Hops and dairying were the farm's main activities, and a double hop kiln and extra dairy were added in this successful period in the farm's life, with a big extension on the south side of the farmhouse to accommodate James Turner's family of eight children.

Tucked away in a barn beside the road, there is a great wooden wagon, over 100 years old, on whose tailboard the painted letters "JAMES TURNER, FARNHAM, SURREY" can still be made out, with a small board on the side bearing the name "C. Turner" — James' son, who succeeded his father in 1903. The wagon was used on journeys to and from Bentley and the surrounding villages, drawn by cart horses which were bred on the farm.

Manley Bridge is no longer a working farm, and its fields are let out for grazing. The barns and dairy are empty, but the house is lived in and cared for, its pleasant Victorian extension facing southwards to the valley, with arched windows, a latticed verandah, and a contemporary matching latticed seat painted pale green, on which generations of the family must have sat to enjoy the sunshine.

The Manley Bridge valley is one of the prettiest corners of "green Farnham".

MANLEY BRIDGE FARM.

23

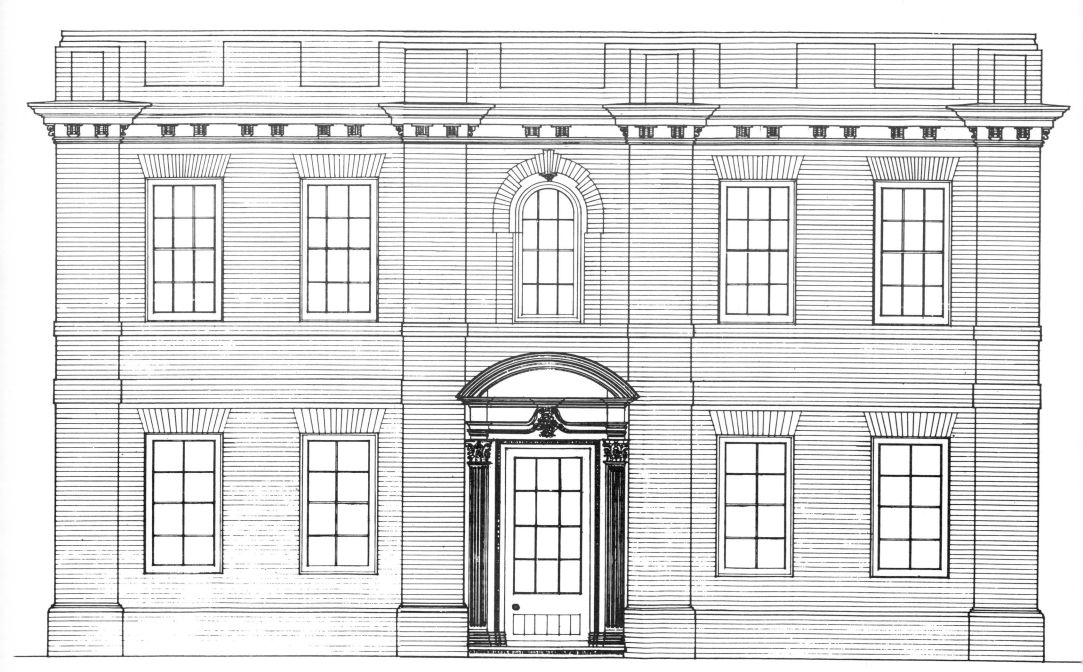

24   THE GRANGE, CASTLE HILL - EAST ELEVATION.

FARNHAM HOUSES

CASTLE STREET - EAST SIDE.

Farnham is famous for its Georgian architecture. This reputation is based on the fact that the town has a rich store of 18th century private houses, and older houses which were refronted in the Georgian style in the same period.

The wave of building which took place in the town in the 18th century arose from local wealth created by two activities, the corn market and the hop-growing industry. The corn market flourished in the 17th century, when for a time Farnham had the biggest market in England for wheat. It declined at the end of the century, to be replaced almost immediately by a rapid increase in hop-growing, which brought even greater wealth to the town throughout the 18th and 19th centuries.

Many large private houses were built in Farnham in the 18th century, starting with The Grange in Castle Hill, Willmer House in West Street, and Weybourne House in Weybourne Road — houses which set the pace for numerous others following in the later years of the century.

Two other factors influenced the development of Farnham in the 19th century — the coming of the railway, and the establishment of the Army in Aldershot. The town continued to be prosperous, and there was a considerable amount of Victorian building on its east and south sides.

Farnham has grown further in the 20th century, and Edwardian development in the southern suburbs has been followed by a sustained gentle expansion in all the surrounding villages, which has gained in intensity in the 1980s.

Thirteen Farnham houses are described in the following pages, a selection of those which have been covered in the **Environmental Viewpoint** articles between 1987 and 1989. They range from a 17th century cottage, through some of the Georgian classics, on to Victorian building and then to some 20th century private houses. The selection is not intended to be comprehensive, but to give a flavour of the architecture of several periods which has made Farnham the place it is.

THE GRANGE

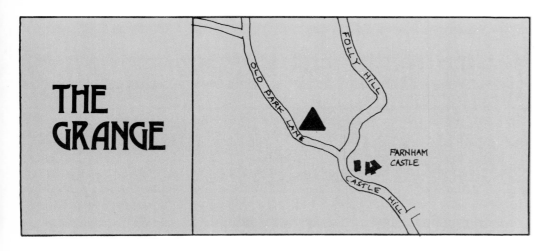

Among more than 400 listed buildings in Farnham, there are only two receiving the distinction of Grade I classification. One of these is Willmer House in West Street (see page 44). The other is The Grange, high on Castle Hill behind its long garden wall, opposite the Castle.

Granges were introduced into England in the early 12th century by the Cistercian Order of Monks. The grange-system of agriculture was designed to achieve efficient food production — principally cereals — at low cost, and The Grange in Farnham today may well stand on the site of the grange of the manor of Farnham first recorded in the early 12th century.

The present house was built in 1709 by Edward Forbes, treasurer and steward to Sir Jonathan Trelawny, Baronet, Bishop of Winchester and Lord of the Manor of Farnham. At the time, part of the Bishop's land had been dis-parked (the Old Park area, extending north and west of the present or New Park, as far as the Hampshire boundary). Edward Forbes converted Old Park into two or three farms, and kept The Grange for his own use.

Even today, with the modern pressure for development in every inch of space, the Old Park area is still open farmland, reaching to within a few hundred yards of West Street and the Hart. The Park itself remained the property of the Bishops of Winchester until the 1930s, when it was bought by Farnham Urban District Council for the people of the town. This green background on the

northern hills of the town so close to the centre, is an extraordinary and potent part of the character of the town today.

The house built by Forbes was surprisingly small, considering its grand style, and it could hardly have been designed for a family. It had only four main rooms (two up and two down) but they were very elegant and spacious with pine panelling, and they were approached by wide panelled corridors and a splendid staircase.

The house is thought to incorporate parts of an earlier "granger's house", because towards its south side, the building contains timber framing and has three storeys, unlike the two storeys of the main house. However, the original south front disappeared when the house was extended by 10 feet in 1907, and it is difficult to be certain.

Today the Grange is square in plan, but not symmetrical. Each of its four facades is different, and each one looks on to a different section of the formal gardens which surround the house. The lawns and flower borders are divided by a quarter of a mile of old brick walls, overgrown with wisteria and ivy and enclosing long garden vistas connected by wrought iron gates.

The house is built of brick, mainly on two floors, and finished with a parapet with a deep wooden cornice running all around the building just below it. The best view is from the east, where the original symmetry of the design is hardly affected by the 20th century extension. It is shown in the drawing without the extension, revealing the classical simplicity of its perfect proportions, with delicate detailing in the windows and brickwork. The doorcase on the east front is one of the finest in Farnham, made of wood with Corinthian pilasters supporting an elliptical pediment.

This side of the house faces a superb garden vista with formal flower beds between clipped yew hedges, and a fountain. It leads towards the Castle and at the end there is a wrought-iron gate between panelled piers of rubbed brick. This grass avenue was once a gravelled path, and must have been the original entrance driveway used by the Bishops coming over from the Castle. This part of the garden used to be known as Buck Close, suggesting an enclosure for deer.

The main entrance to The Grange is on the west side, approached from Old Park Lane. The front door has a heavy canopy supported by brackets, facing a gravel drive which circles around an Irish yew tree. In the original design, the west front was symmetrical, with five bays and the door in the centre, but this was lost when a sixth bay was added in the 20th century extension to the south front.

The kitchen entrance, within the extension, faces south and here the building has three storeys. The north facade has only three bays with sashed windows around a plain door, looking on to a walled garden with a tiny summerhouse at the far end.

Inside, the entrance hall is panelled in red pine which has been stripped and polished. The floor is made of white chalk stone which was probably taken from the ruined walls of the Castle, and at the end of the hall an oak staircase leads to the first floor gallery. The stair well is decorated with three remarkable painted murals, possibly the work of Sir James Thornhill, dated between 1720 and 1740, depicting allegorical scenes contained within "trompe l'oeuil" painted marble pilasters and festoons.

At the beginning of the 20th century, The Grange was neglected and dilapidated. It had been leased to a hop-farmer called Charles Andrews, but when he died in 1906 the house was bought by George and Emily Johnson, drapers of Downing Street, who did a lot of repair and rebuilding, including the extension of the south front. Since 1919 the house has had only two owners.

The Grade I listing of the Grange is justified by its impressive rectangular plan surrounded by formal garden vistas, its classic early Georgian design, and its 18th century murals around the stair well. Its deeply rooted historical associations with the Bishops of Winchester and the life of the town, together with its superb position between the Castle and the rolling farmland of Old Park, make it one of Farnham's most important houses.

Michael Blower

THE GRANGE - EAST DOOR.

27

2 DOWNING STREET

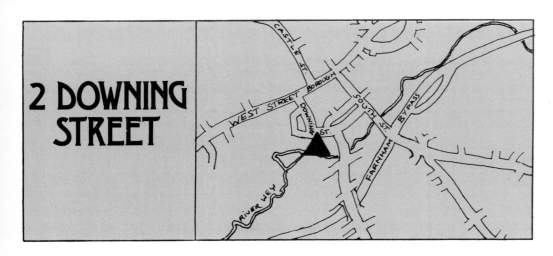

As the name suggests, Downing Street led in medieval Farnham down to the wide shallow river crossing at Longbridge. (The requirements of a modern one-way traffic system have changed this, and perhaps the street should be re-named Upping Street!)

At the lower end of Downing Street where it turns eastwards and widens out, there is an interesting group of houses with their backs to the river, of a much more expansive style and scale than the cottages opposite.

2 Downing Street is the end building, next to the Police Station. Its present name is Boardman House, but in the past it has been known as Morley House and as Rhama House. It stands a little way back from the road behind a paved forecourt, with steps leading to the front door.

The main facade of 2 Downing Street is contained by a projecting wing on the east side, and by the side of 3 Downing Street on the west. Both these are in red brick, framing the yellow brick facade of No 2 with gentle contrast. The facade is early Victorian (1830 or just after) but it still follows the Georgian tradition so successfully practised elsewhere in Farnham, with a classically symmetrical 3-bay design and a central door. The

DOOR AT 2, DOWNING STREET

NOS 2 & 2B DOWNING STREET

facade is divided horizontally by a stone string course, and by a stone cornice supported at each end by ornamental brackets. The parapet is neatly stepped up in the centre, and the pale yellow-grey bricks, together with cream-coloured stone, blend harmoniously with the surrounding red brick.

But this elegant Victorian facade is very far from being the whole story at 2 Downing Street. Behind it there is the greater part of an older red brick building, probably late medieval, standing several feet further away from the road than the present one. This older house was refronted and almost entirely remodelled when the 1830 facade was added, although some of the original roof timbers remain *in situ*.

The drawings record recent changes at the back of the house. From a medieval timber-framed building with a long garden reaching to the river, to a house of Victorian appearance, through to a modern office block — which is the use of the building today — 2 Downing Street has experienced many transformations.

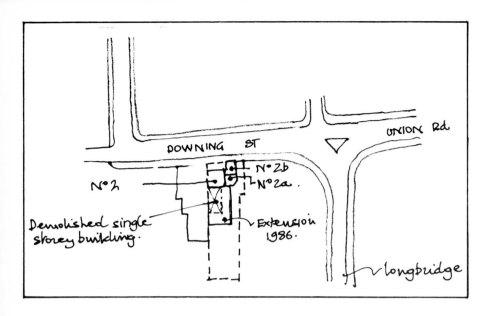

PLAN SHOWING CHANGES AT 2 DOWNING STREET.
AN OLD SINGLE STOREY EXTENSION AT THE REAR WAS
REPLACED BY A LARGER ONE IN 1986.

M Blower May '86

ENTRANCE TO 2A. DOWNING STREET, DRAWN IN 1986.

REBUILDING IN PROGRESS AT REAR OF 2 DOWNING STREET, 1986.

EXTENSION AT REAR OF 2 DOWNING STREET, 1988.

M Blower

THE RANGER'S HOUSE

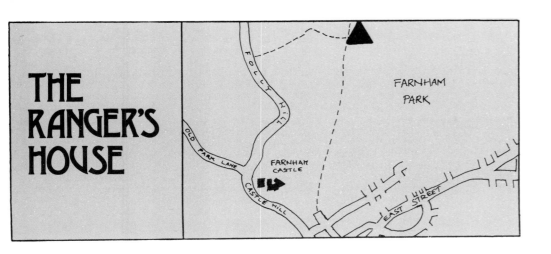

Some years after the end of World War II, the Ranger's House had a very narrow escape from demolition. From the perspective of the more conservation-oriented 1980s, this is hard to believe. Yet it very nearly happened.

The Ranger's House was built in the early 18th century as a lodging for the Ranger of Farnham Park who was employed by the Bishop of Winchester at Farnham Castle. At this time, the Old Park area to the north and west had recently been dis-parked and enclosed for farming, and the Ranger would have been responsible for the 300 acres of the New Park (the present park) extending eastwards towards Hale. According to a local tradition, the first occupant of the Ranger's House was a member of the well-known local Vernon family who owned important property in West Street.

During the war, the Ranger's house was a Home Guard post, and it was surrounded by tall brick blast walls built so close to the walls of the house that there was only just room to squeeze in between. After the war, the house, which belonged like the Park itself to Farnham Urban District Council, stood empty for several years. In 1957 the Council proposed to pull it down, but it was saved by a joint effort on the part of the Farnham Society and its chairman Richard Dufty, and the Society for the Protection of Ancient Buildings supported by John Betjeman. It was advertised to let under a full repairing lease, and within days tenants were found who still live in the house today.

The new occupants were Sir Brooks and Lady Richards, who undertook the very extensive work necessary to repair, restore and modernise the house. They put cornices and decorated chimney pieces into the three main ground floor rooms, replaced missing doors with doors from a demolished house in Lincolnshire, and created a new front door in place of the original kitchen entrance, inserting an 18th century door with a hood supported by scroll brackets.

The result is a house of distinction and charm, an asset to the Park and to the town. The debt owed to the occupiers and to those whose determination saved the house from annihilation is great.

THE RANGER'S HOUSE,   FARNHAM PARK.

34

THE BRIDGE HOUSE

Visitors to Farnham may be puzzled to see a painted sign on the side of a house in Longbridge, saying "Reid & Co's Ales & Stout". The house is obviously not a pub, so why the sign?

The answer is that this was The Bridge House Inn, although only for a short period between 1850 and 1902. It then became one of the victims of an attempt by the local Bench to rectify a situation described by a contemporary writer who said of Farnham that "Shocking scenes of drunkenness and debauchery were enacted in the town". In 1902, the renewal of the licences of nine local pubs was refused, a precedent which was later followed throughout the country, resulting in the closing of a third of the pubs in Britain. By 1914, Farnham had lost 20 pubs, and more disappeared in succeeding years. (Whether this has cured the problem or not is a matter for speculation.)

The Bridge House Inn occupied the part of the house nearest to the river, which is a mid-19th century addition to a much older, possibly 16th century house. This older part consists of a small section sandwiched between later buildings, with the 19th century ex-pub on the river side, and on the other some premises which were rebuilt at the turn of the century when Bridge Square was enlarged. The older building can be distinguished by its height, a small gable end standing directly against the pavement, and roofed with old tiles in contrast to the modern grey ones on the roofs nearer the river.

The old building is taller than its neighbours. It has in fact got three storeys although this is not apparent from the front, where only a ground floor and an upper floor window are visible. The

THE BRIDGE HOUSE, FROM LONGBRIDGE.

Michael Blower

THE BRIDGE HOUSE, FROM ITS GARDEN.

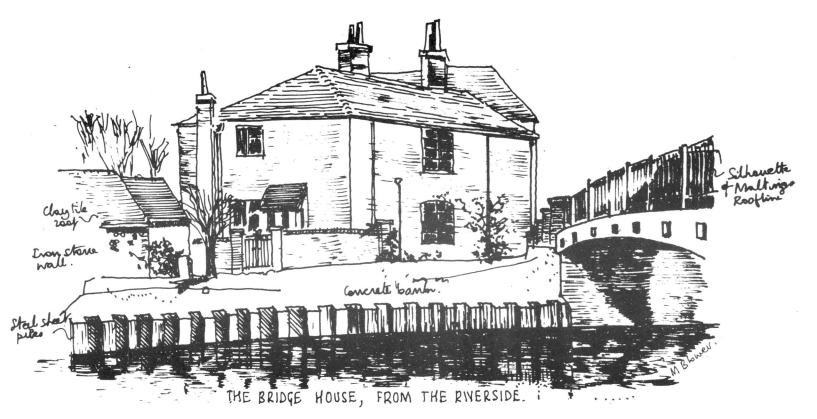

Clay tile roof

Iron stone wall.

Steel sheet piles

Concrete banker.

Silhouette of Maltings Roofline

M Bowen.

THE BRIDGE HOUSE, FROM THE RIVERSIDE.

disparity occurred when the ceiling between the ground and first floor room at the front was removed to compensate for a loss of height after the level of the floor had been raised by about 2 feet. The result is an extraordinarily high room with a cupboard in the wall 12 feet up, quite unreachable unless by ladder. Even more surprising, the room is overlooked by a first floor window surviving from the older house, which is now inside the building and looks on to a landing.

The combination of a very old building with a later one on a confined site between the bridge and the river has produced a very unusual house. From the inside, it divides itself distinctly between the old and the newer sections. Each part has its own staircase — both dizzily steep and narrow — and the rooms are full of corners and steps accommodating all the changes of level.

The 19th century part is shaped like a wedge of cheese — angled away from the old house towards the river, and ending in a corner much closer to 45° than 90° where it meets the back of the house. This curious dimension creates odd-shaped rooms with inaccessible corners, but its unusual features make The Bridge House very memorable. It has a unique position beside the river crossing — looking out across the roofs of the town — with a view of the Castle from its bathroom window.

Since it ceased to be a pub, The Bridge House has been owned and lived in by a single family, the Cranstones. The front room next to the bridge used to be a little general shop run by Mrs Cranstone, and for 80 years the house has been loved and cherished by this one family. What an unusual situation for our modern times, when such continuity is rare.

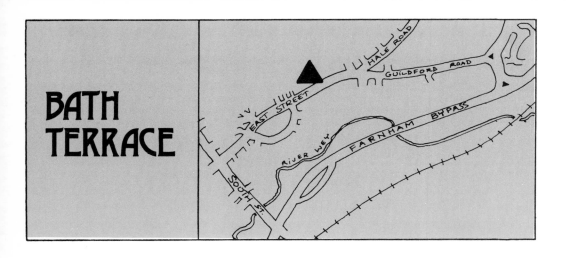

BATH TERRACE

Unlike Georgian West Street and Castle Street, East Street expanded as a result of the Victorian growth spurt, when fields and hopgrounds were sold off for new housing estates. Between East Street and the southern slopes of the Park, there is some extremely attractive Victorian development, interspersed with tiny yards and alleys leading away from the street and up the hill.

East Street has been roughly treated in recent years, from the building of the unloved Woolmead of the '60s and early '70s, to the shattering of the street scene which resulted from the driving through of the characterless Dogflud Way. This joyless race-track runs behind the sheds of the Swain & Jones 'island', past a recent eruption of brown industrial buildings and the uncompromisingly stark Sports Centre (mercifully being rapidly hidden by trees) and back into East Street, opening up views of the unkempt sides of chopped-off buildings.

In the face of this insensitive development which alienates East Street from the rest of the town centre and the conservation area, it is all the more important to appreciate the attractive buildings which have survived the onslaught. Opposite the eastern end of Dogflud Way there is a group of demurely white-clad Victorian or Edwardian villas, where evergreen shrubs — laurel and fir — in the small front gardens make a pretty picture.

Moving eastwards past the massive dark bulk of St James's Church (converted into flats) one comes to the tall white-fronted building which was built as Bath Terrace by William Patrick in 1847, now Bath House and West Meon House. It has an elongated form, with three storeys plus a basement area, and it is separated from the road by two tiny front gardens with brick pillars and iron railings. The front of the house is cemented and painted white, the shallow pitched roof is of slate, and there is a brick chimney running through the centre. The sashed windows are well-proportioned, and the two front doors, placed at the extreme edges of the façade and reached by a flight of steps, have semi-circular fanlights with a radial tracery design, and cement-cased surrounds.

This Victorian house is unusual in Farnham, where cellars are much more usual than basement areas, and the very marked division of what would otherwise be a façade with a considerable amount of Georgian style is also surprising. The separation is strengthened by the positioning of the two doors as far away from each other as they could possibly be, and by the vertical line of the central chimney stack.

Curiously, the exposed western flank of the house, which is without windows, is of ironstone while the front is white-painted cement and the east side and back are of white 'clunch' chalkstone with brick dressings. On each side of the house, clunch-built garden walls rise with the slope of the ground in a sweeping curve, and the east side of the house, where a footpath leads up towards Stoke Hills, is framed by a clump of trees.

Victorian East Street was not included when the Farnham Conservation Area was designated, and it is easy to forget its attractions among Farnham's more famous features. It deserves more recognition.

BATH TERRACE, EAST STREET.

39

THE CHESTNUTS

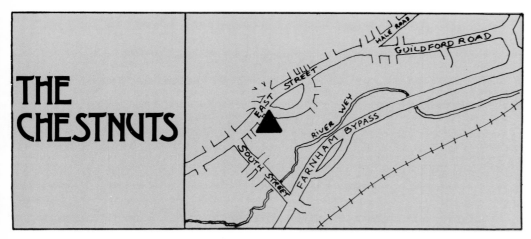

Of the streets in Farnham town centre, East Street is the one to have been most changed in recent years. The '60s and early '70s brought a radical reconstruction of a large area near the junction with the Borough, resulting in the Woolmead development and a new loop road around its back. In the '80s another new loop road, Dogflud Way, which leads to the Riverside Park Industrial estate and the Sports Centre, was added, and in 1988 the 1930s Regal Cinema was demolished, leaving a gaping space which remained empty for more than two years.

These changes have left East Street battered and battle-scarred, disjointed and bereft of its identity. In this setting, it is nice to find a building which, although it has suffered alteration and neglect in the last 50 years, has now been restored and given a street presence which has a benevolent influence on its jagged surroundings.

The Chestnuts stands on a corner site at the point where Brightwells Road meets East Street, next to the large rectangular plot which used to be occupied by the bulky brick form of the Regal Cinema. In the early years of this century the Chestnuts was owned by Admiral Molteno, but in 1935 after the cinema opened next door he sold it to Farnham Urban District Council,

GARDENS BEHIND THE CHESTNUTS, DRAWN IN 1976.

The Chestnuts. East St. Pham.

MB Lowry Feb '88

finding his new neighbour rather too large and busy for his comfort. With its long garden at the back, it was at first suggested that the house would be an ideal place for a library or museum, but instead it eventually became the local employment exchange, and a new Health Centre was built at the end of the garden.

The front of The Chestnuts used to be in line with other frontages in East Street, but shortly after the war there was a serious fire which caused so much damage that the front had to be rebuilt, and the line was taken back to its present position, chopping off the front part of the building. The reason was that at the time there was a plan to do the same with other properties on that side of East Street, in order to widen it, but this did not happen and the result is that the area in front of the Chestnuts, previously a small garden, has now been paved and planted with trees to form a very pleasant open space. The new trees are, of course, chestnuts.

Before 1987-88, when the latest renovation was done, The Chestnuts had become very dilapidated. The building had only a single storey at the back, and the gardens behind it were overgrown, with crumbling walls, tumbledown sheds, and piles of rubbish.

Now, the strong symmetrical brick East Street facade, parapeted above five bays with well-proportioned sash windows and a central door, has been very well restored. The small matching extension on the east side, which shares the roof of the main building, sets off the brick facade pleasantly with its cream-painted rendering and brick quoins and takes its place neatly in the street line.

At the back, an upper floor has been added, again with cream-painted rendering above the existing brick ground floor. Here the most interesting feature is the handsome doorcase which has been meticulously repaired and restored. Its fluted pilasters surmounted by a semi-circular fanlight with six rounded segments, and pediment with dentil ornament, create an effect of lightness and delicacy.

DOOR AT THE REAR OF THE CHESTNUTS

REAR VIEW OF THE CHESTNUTS BEFORE RESTORATION.

M Blower 18th Dec 1985.

The renovation of The Chestnuts was given a Farnham Society Amenity Award in 1988, and the blue metal plaque can be seen fixed to the front of the building. It recognises a highly successful piece of conservation, in which the temptation to demolish a fragile old building and rebuild on a cleared site has been resisted, and the scale and presence of an older building retained in a way which is seldom achieved with a new one. This principle of making use of the legacy of the past, instead of obliterating it, is of the greatest importance in Farnham where the character of the town depends as much on its small or semi-industrial old buildings as on its great houses and noble architecture. Their loss diminishes the town's character.

WILLMER HOUSE

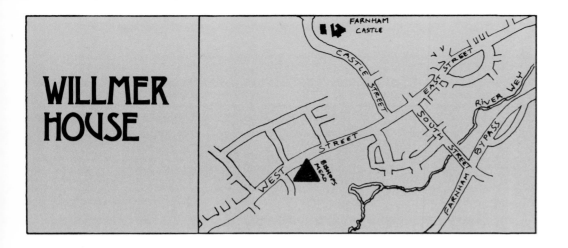

Willmer House, 38 West Street, is one of the two buildings in Farnham to achieve the rare distinction of Grade I listing. The other is The Grange in Castle Street (see page 26).

At first sight, the reason for this status may not be apparent. Willmer House was built in 1718, standing directly on the road, without any ostentatious features or obvious grandeur. Its special quality lies in the design and execution of the front facade, which earns high praise from Pevsner and Nairn who describe it as "one of the finest cut brick facades in the country".

The front of Willmer House is symmetrical and almost square. It has five bays and three full floors and is constructed of cut and gauged bricks of an unusually high standard of workmanship. No coarse brick at all has been used in the construction. Instead, each individual brick has been rubbed to create a fine texture and a smooth sophisticated finish. The joints between the bricks are pencil-thin and finely executed, using lime mortar. This is local craftsmanship at its best, but its quality indicates that the conception can hardly have been the result of a country craftsman's intuition alone.

In the design, the horizontal and the vertical are very evenly balanced. The horizontals are formed by the plinth, the moulded string course between the windows, the cornice, and the panelled parapet with moulded coping. The verticals are represented by the fourteen tall sash windows, closely set, the slight forward projection of the central bay, and most of all by the giant brick pilasters at the two outer angles of the building, running its full 30 foot height and forming a frame which visually binds the structure.

The detail of one of the brick pilasters is shown opposite. The pattern of the brickwork is made up of a sequence repeated all the way from plinth to cornice, consisting of four courses followed by one recessed course which creates a regular shadowed underlining of each sequence and gives the pilasters their visual impact.

Within this overall pattern there is an inner rhythm created by the way the bricks are laid, in a sequence using stretchers (bricks laid with the long side visible), headers (bricks laid end on) and closers (headers cut in half).

The pattern consists of blocks of four brick courses following a 'rhyme scheme' like that of a poem, with a sequence of alternating 'verses' all the way up the pilaster created by variations of stretchers, headers and closers. This subtlety, however, is not purely decorative; like all good design it is functional, and the closers are mathematically necessary in order to maintain the geometry in three dimensions of the corner of the building, because they represent the third element which achieves the bonding.

Willmer House was built in 1718, just nine years later than The Grange in Castle Hill. It is said to have been sold in 1723 for £523. In the 19th century, Miss Willmer's boarding house for young ladies was established there, giving the house the name by which it is known today, and this educational tradition was revived in 1960 when the building was acquired by Farnham Urban District Council who made it into Farnham Museum.

THE FACADE OF WILLMER HOUSE.

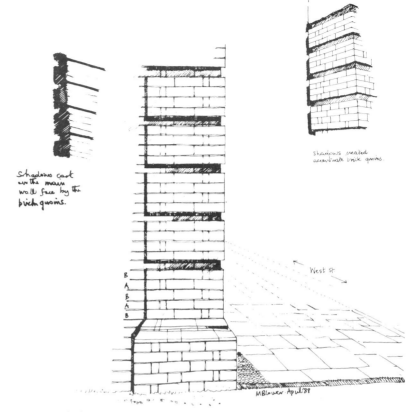

Shadows cast on the main wall face by the brick quoins.

Shadows created accentuate brick quoins.

West St

WILLMER HOUSE - DETAIL OF BRICKWORK.

Willmer House is of course open to the public, and it is a fascinating place to visit with exhibitions and a library of books on local history in its panelled rooms. Passing through the building, the visitor walks into a walled garden bright with flowers, to reach a small gallery at the far end. It is a most delightful place.

In the cluster of great Georgian houses in West Street, Willmer House is neither the largest nor the grandest, but the brilliance of its design and the high standard of the craftsmanship which went into its construction, make it in its own quiet way outstanding.

THE OLD HOUSE, WEYBOURNE.

46

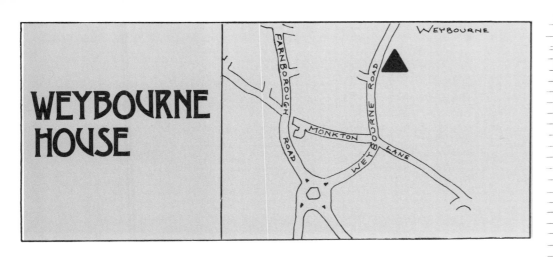

WEYBOURNE HOUSE

One of the first Georgian private houses to be built in Farnham, and a member of that early group which set the pace for Georgian building in the district for many years, is Weybourne House.

It is quite a surprise to come upon this imposing classically designed residence in the modern setting of Weybourne Road. In the approach from Farnham, its west front shows a distinctive outline created by the ornamentally shaped chimney which stands high on the parapet, above a froth of greenery in the garden below, but it is quite easy to miss, simply because unless one knows it is there it is very unexpected.

The house is thought to be by Peter Coldham, built in 1729, and this date appears on two lead rainwater hoppers on the west front. It is built of brick, parapeted and tiled, and it is said that it contains some of the fabric of the ruined Waverley Abbey which was owned by the Coldham family from 1609 until its sale to John Aislabie in the 1720s.

In the 19th century, Weybourne House was owned by the Knight family, and John Henry Knight, famous for his mechanical inventions including one of the earliest motor cars. was born here in 1847. He lived in the house until moving to Barfield in Runfold in 1888. In 1947 the house was bought by Farnham Urban District Council.

WEYBOURNE HOUSE - FRONT DOOR.

When Weybourne House was first built the road was slightly closer than it is today, following recent road re-alignment. It stands behind tall horse chestnut trees which in summer partly hide its symmetrical facade of five bays, built throughout of brick with the only other material being the wood of the door and window frames. The windows are sashed and surmounted by segmented arches of rubbed bricks, and there is a projecting band course between the ground and first floor windows including a moulded brick course which is possibly unique in Farnham.

The central feature of the facade is a slightly projecting section in which the door and one window are set, which runs the full height of the house. This section has been executed in cut brickwork similar to that in Willmer House at 38 West Street, built ten years earlier. The bricks have been reduced in size by rubbing down, with very fine joints and a sophisticated smooth finish. The precision of this treatment achieves the perfect measures necessary to the delicate geometry of the design.

The design of the central projection provides a focus within which the doorcase displays the meticulous attention typically devoted to such features in houses of the period. It is strongly modelled with moulding, cornice, frieze and architrave, all in brick, and it exemplifies the way in which 18th century architecture achieved individuality within the constraints of classical design and rule through the variety of arrangement of elements in the facade, especially in the treatment of windows and design of doorways. This technique was especially evident in provincial houses, and it gave them the pleasant and friendly character which is very noticeable in Weybourne Old House.

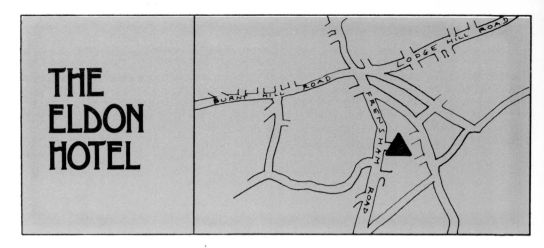

THE ELDON HOTEL

Out on the A287 Frensham Road, beyond the Bourne crossroads, is an Edwardian family house whose comforts have been enjoyed by thousands of people. This is the Eldon Hotel, for many years a familiar part of life in Farnham, but threatened in 1989 with demolition and replacement with 35 sheltered housing units.

As the private house which it was originally, the building was not particularly large or grand. It was built in a typical Edwardian style with gables and a balcony, in brick and pebbledash with some tile-hanging, with a large front garden and a drive to a small matching garage at the back.

Its most interesting features are its tiles and chimneys. Ornamental curved tiles have been used on all the roofs, and looped ridge tiles at the apex are silhouetted against the sky. The chimneys are unusually slender, decorated with a vertical brick pattern which emphasises the upward sweep, and widening with decorative brickwork at the top.

To cater for its existence as a hotel, various alterations were made. Several extensions were added to one side of the building, and the original front door was replaced by a new hotel entrance.

The care evidently taken in the design and detailed finish of what must have been a relatively modest family house, is very pleasing. It is a reminder of an age when craftsmen were plentiful and labour was cheaper, and there was time for those individual finishing touches which give a house its personality.

The Eldon Hotel. De Bourne. Farnham.

Michael Blower 2E Dec'88

THE OLD COTTAGE

The Old Cottage is some distance from the road, up a steep and narrow pathway between trees and shrubs. The oldest part of the house is 17th century, with an 18th century addition and a later outshot at the back, giving it three distinct sections. There is a cellar under the 18th century part which may be older than the building above it.

Alma Lane in Heath End is perhaps not often thought of as a place with a history. The road looks very modern, bordered with new building, and as the A3016, part of the National Primary Route Network carrying traffic between the M3 and Guildford, it is very busy.

In fact, though, the origins of Alma Lane go back to Saxon times when it was part of an ancient route running from Odiham through Heath End, and on via what is now Weybourne Lane to Runfold and Crooksbury. The modern name was given to the road 60 years ago when local roads were being named after First World War battles. Before that, it had been Ayling Lane, from the Saxon word meaning "the home of Aegel".

Despite its modern appearance, Alma Lane has some very old houses. Hidden behind laurels and fir trees, on a bend in the road almost opposite the Alma public house, is "The Old Cottage", once part of a small settlement on land at Lawday Common, Bricksbury Hill and Hungry Hill. The Old Cottage, with Yonder Cottage next to it and Beam Cottage opposite, are the only survivors from this group because most of the houses disappeared when the Army took over the land to the north.

M B Blower
Jan 1988.

THE OLD COTTAGE - INTERIOR.

THE OLD COTTAGE. ALMA LANE

M Blower
Jan 88

The walls of the house are pebbledashed and whitewashed over brick, the windows are small, the roof is of warm red tiles, and there are three whitewashed chimneys, one at each end and one in the middle. On the south side of the house a verandah was added in the 19th century, but only part of it now remains.

Before the Army came to Aldershot in the mid-19th century, the Old Cottage was known as Crescent Cottages and was lived in by Edward Harrington, a labourer and a member of a large and well-known local family. Later, the house became one of several locally which catered to the needs of soldiers, serving as a laundry and as a beer house. For a time it was a licensed public house, called first The Light Horse, and later The Flying Fox.

19th century owners of The Old Cottage included some well-known names such as Mr W.J. Hollest and Mr George Trimmer. The house ceased to be a pub, and became two cottages, in about 1890, and it was given its present name in 1936 by the Misses Agnes Eide and Annie Snowball, who lived in the house until 1962 and did a lot of restoration work.

The present owners, have done a great deal of research into the history of the house and the surrounding area, and have speculated romantically about its connections with Dick Turpin who is known to have frequented the area. Who would have thought that such exciting imaginings could lie behind the hedges of modern Alma Lane?

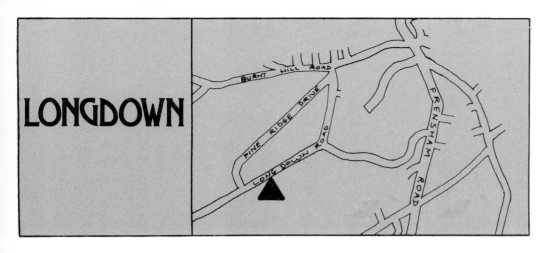

LONGDOWN

Longdown Road crosses hilly country between Burnt Hill Road and Gardeners Hill Road, linking the Bourne and Boundstone. There are houses on both sides of the road, but they are widely spaced out and set back, and the scene is rural. The road dips and climbs through thick growths of the trees which love the local sandy soil — the evergreen pine and fir, with oak, beech, birch, and clumps of the purple-flowered naturalised rhododendron.

Building in Longdown Road is all relatively recent, following after the enclosure of common lands in the 19th century at a time when development in the South Farnham hills was gaining momentum. The south side of the road, edged by steep banks and sharp slopes, with its breath-taking views, must always have been an attraction for architects and their clients, because it offers such dramatic sites for building.

"Longdown", at 20 Longdown Road, has just such a site. It is on ground which slopes down away from the road, and its south-facing windows look on to acres of rolling woodland, with hardly a building to be seen, even today. The garden drops sharply away behind the house, with clumps of daffodils in spring competing with the native heather among rhododendrons and azaleas.

The house is three storeys high, giving extra height to compensate for the fact that it stands almost four feet below the level of the road. The road front possesses very striking originality of design, clearly the work of an architect with an unconventional cast of mind, but its development is puzzling.

It appears that when it was first built, Longdown was quite a small house, but that it was substantially altered and extended in the first decade of this century. Originally it was about two-thirds of its present size, three storeys high as now, with a gabled entrance porch which was only about half the height of the present one.

In 1904 (if a note bearing that date, recently discovered at the back of a cupboard, is an indication) someone took this quite simple house and turned it into something out of the ordinary. There is a suggestion, unconfirmed, that it may have been the work of the London architect W. Curtis Green who was born nearby in Alton and who carried out some work in the Farnham area. The Church of the Good Shepherd in Dockenfield is by him.

When the house was altered, a large extension was added on the west side with a new chimney running down through the middle of the house to provide a raised double-sided hearth between two ground-floor rooms. The new roof was pulled out sharply sideways in a flaring line, its lower edge underscored by square cast-iron guttering with a design of oak leaves and acorns. The exaggeratedly tall chimney was decorated with a pattern of dancing rectangles worked in dark brick against the red. Perhaps to balance the horizontal emphasis of the sideways-extended new roof, the entrance porch was raised by an extra storey to form a tower, with a tiny room inside it. Later, the entrance was moved, and the present square entrance porch does not appear to be part of the same design.

Until quite recently, there was a sunken garden in front of the house, approached through a gate in the wall and down a flight of steps, but this has been filled in to provide an entrance for cars at road level, and the lower part of the house walls are obscured.

Unconventional — imaginative — perhaps eccentric and certainly puzzling — Longdown is a house that lingers in the memory.

LONGDOWN

53

1 FRENSHAM ROAD

When you have lived in a town for a number of years, you may think you know it quite well. In fact this is never really true: what you know is what you can see from the street, and attractive buildings and views can exist, close to the busy road but hidden from it and unseen by passers-by.

1 Frensham Road is such a house. It is close to the Ridgway traffic lights, tucked away between St Thomas's Church and the reservoir, on lower ground behind a high bank and hedge, with only its chimneys visible from the road. It is a big house, standing in nearly an acre of garden, approached down a steeply sloping drive at the side of the plot. A dense belt of evergreen trees separates the drive from the garden, which is entered through an arch of greenery and down some steps.

The front garden opens out immediately, a flat square of ground with gravel paths intersecting flowerbeds each neatly framed with old-fashioned box hedges.

The house, built some 60 or so years ago, is in a vernacular 'cottage' idiom with white rough-cast walls under a brown tiled roof. Its most striking feature is the use of horizontal bands of small mullioned windows in groups of unequal length, complementing the long horizontal roof lines. In contrast, a broad central gable bisects the length of the house at the front.

This gable, with a wooden 'stable door' is unusually wide, and its side walls are not perpendicular but fractionally bowed, giving it a slightly pregnant look.

This house has an earthy feeling about it, deeply bedded and rooted in its garden and built of natural traditional materials — earth-coloured tiles, soft-textured rough-cast, dark wood and hand-crafted ironwork. It has a big garden, a wide lawn with flowering trees, an orchard, a fishpond sheltered by yew hedges, and in spring a sapphire sweep of bluebells colours the bank under the trees. It is the sort of house, with its interesting design and spacious setting, which makes residential South Farnham the pleasant place it is.

This description, and the drawing, records 1 Frensham Road as it was in the spring of 1989. At the time, the house was empty and there were planning applications being considered, one for a new house to be built in the garden, the other for demolition of the house and its replacement by two blocks of flats, one of them three storeys high, with parking for 24 cars in the garden.

This embodies the planning dilemma which causes so much heart-ache in Farnham in the 1980s. Should established residential areas like South Farnham, with houses of interesting design and large gardens around them, experience the inevitable change of character which follows when big houses are pulled down and replaced with high density development? Looking at 1 Frensham Road in its lovely garden, the prospect fills one with sadness.

1, FRENSHAM ROAD.

HALE PLACE.

M.Blower. June 26th 1988

56

HALE PLACE

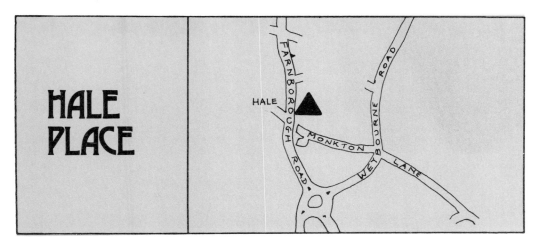

Hale Place is one of a group of older buildings around the Hale Road / Farnborough Road crossroads beside St John's Church. The house fell on hard times after it was sold in the mid-1980s, standing empty for several years, and in 1988 when these drawings were done it was in a sad state. Its gates were barricaded, and its windows boarded up and blank. The lawn was high and rank with weeds, rubbish lay under the bushes, and a section of balustrade from the first floor balcony of the house had fallen on to the terrace below. Lead had been stripped from the porch, and slates and ridge tiles were missing from the out-buildings, leaving holes open to the weather.

When the house was built in the first half of the 19th century it was a substantial family house, on its sunny south-facing slope with gardens and grounds of exceptional quality, and superb views towards Crooksbury. A water colour painting dated 1859 shows the house against a luxuriant shelter of trees, a compact and pleasant place in white stucco, with shuttered windows under slate roofs. There was a coach house and stables on the east side, across a large yard, and in 1853 Hale Place was owned by Henry Sellwood, father-in-law of the poet Tennyson who is believed to have been an occasional visitor.

OUTBUILDINGS AT HALE PLACE.

57

THE WALLED GARDEN AT HALE PLACE.

In succeeding years, new wings were added to the east and west of the original house, giving it its present slightly disjointed appearance, but its best feature is its entrancing gardens with magnificent trees, a sweeping expanse of lawn, and a sun-trap of a kitchen garden surrounded by soft-hued brick walls which look as though they pre-date the house itself.

Despite its neglected condition in 1988, Hale Place still possessed the dignity imparted by its superb grounds. The kitchen garden still had fruit trees espaliered against the old brick walls, and climbing roses hanging in festoons over the arched gateways framing glorious southerly views. Raspberries still grew in the fruit cage, but the vegetable plots, edged with low box hedges, had been taken over by clumps of thistle and patches of poppies, daisies and blue cranesbill.

After Hale Place changed hands in the mid-1980s, a planning application was put in proposing conversion of the house to flats with new maisonettes built in the garden. After lengthy negotiation, it was agreed that the walls of the old kitchen garden would not be demolished, and a planning consent was eventually obtained. During this process, the Department of the Environment considered a proposal that the house should be listed, to save it from the demolition which became an increasing threat as it deteriorated during the long period when it was empty. Unfortunately, the decision was that the house did not meet the required architectural standards, and this is a pity because it is often precisely the houses like Hale Place, admittedly not of the highest quality architecturally yet important historically and in their setting, which need the protection of listing.

FARNHAM STREET SCENES

UNION ROAD.

If it was the river in its hospitable valley which attracted Farnham's first inhabitants in prehistoric times, it was the road — the east-west trading route to the coast — which was the largest factor in the town's development. The first track was called the Harrow Way, leading in the pre-Christian period from Stonehenge across the Hampshire Downs, through Farnham and on to the Hog's Back. Part of this road later became the Pilgrims Way.

When the Saxon king Cedwalla gave Farnham to the Church by Charter in 688, the town was already prosperous. The Norman castle, built in 1138, provided a dwelling place for the Bishop half way between Winchester and London, and it was placed on a hill overlooking the crossing point of the important roads.

The Borough, at the foot of the hill below the Castle, was enclosed by a ditch and a fence, and was quite small, with its east gate by the Bush and its west gate at the top of Downing Street. Houses grew up near the church and also along West Street, which was the road to the coast. Downing Street led down to the river and to Abbey Street (the road to Waverley Abbey), and the King's Highway led east to London through the district known as Dogflud. South of the river, tracks led to Wrecclesham, Frensham and Elstead, and north of the Castle, to Odiham.

This medieval road pattern is little changed in Farnham today, apart from the addition of South Street and Union Road in the 19th century. To the south, the town has expanded towards the villages of The Bourne and Boundstone, and development has spread eastwards to join Hale and Heath End, but there are few roads in the farming land to the north-west and this has kept development there to a minimum.

In the pages which follow, a variety of street scenes are described, both in the town centre and in its outer suburbs. The subjects range from the well-known historic areas such as Bridge Square and the Church Lanes; to a study of changes in South Street; to a history of The Bush Hotel; to some out-of-town shops; and to the famous wheelwright's shop written about by the Farnham author George Sturt. This section of the book, and the book itself, ends with a view of the town's most famous street, Castle Street.

60   THE WILLIAM COBBETT PUBLIC HOUSE, BRIDGE SQUARE.

ABBEY STREET & BRIDGE SQUARE

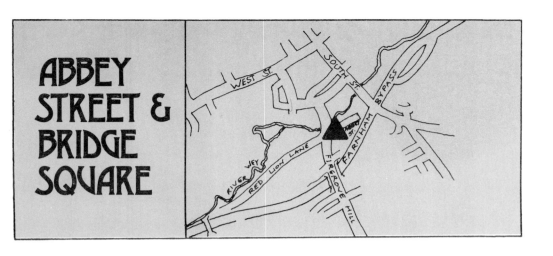

Abbey Street received its name because it led to Waverley Abbey, built two miles outside the town, near the River Wey, in 1128. Pilgrims and visitors would go along Downing Street to the Longbridge, and through Abbey Street to make their way south-eastwards to the abbey.

In the 1940s, Abbey Street was actually part of the main route through Farnham, connecting the two parts of the bypass which had been built before the war, via Bridge Square and Red Lion Lane.

But in spite of its historic importance, Abbey Street is not part of the modern traffic system. When the bypass was widened at Hickley's Corner and the present traffic lights installed, the eastern end of Abbey Street was closed, and it now peters out unsatisfactorily under the high bank which shelters it from the bypass. Buildings on the corner of Abbey Street and South Street, including the three-storey Hickley's building, were demolished to make room for the road.

Abbey Street now has a split personality. At the South Street end there is large-scale new building, the Providence Place old people's flats and the huge Hickley's Court office development dominating the corner beside the traffic lights. At the Bridge Square end, the street is within the Farnham Conservation Area, with old cottages lining its southern side, and the William Cobbett public house on the corner. The dichotomy is illustrated in the drawing done in August 1987, showing the paraphernalia of construction work in the foreground, with a curve of old buildings in the distance.

Abbey Street used to have three pubs — the Jolly Farmer, which was re-named the William Cobbett in the 1940s; the Lamb; and the Bricklayers Arms whose licence was transferred in 1939 to a new building in Weydon Lane. Houses on the north side of Abbey Street, at the Bridge Square end, were designed by the architect Thomas Wonnacott, a dissenter and temperance campaigner, who built the Congregational Church in South Street in 1872, and at his insistence, the houses in Abbey Street were covered by a covenant forbidding their use as public houses.

Probably the most famous view in Farnham is the William Cobbett public house against its high bank, as it is seen from

ABBEY STREET IN 1987.

outside the police station, looking across the bridge with the Maltings on one side and Bridge House on the other. This view seems to sum up so much of the town's character — its river, its red-brick and timber-framed buildings, and its atmosphere of rural serenity.

Ironically, though, this much-reproduced view has seen many changes over the years. In the 17th century a long 6-span wooden bridge formed the crossing over the river, replaced in 1853 by a single-span iron bridge when traffic from the south side of the town began to increase, following the opening of the

railway. Until 1971, there was still a ford to the west of the bridge beside the Maltings, with a gently sloping pathway leading to the river on each side, but the bridge was rebuilt and widened, and the picturesque ford had to go. The police station was built in 1963 on the site of a house and builders' yard.

The appearance of the pub has changed, too. Forty years ago, called the Jolly Farmer, it was stuccoed and painted white, but when the plaster was removed during re-decoration, revealing the warm red brick underneath, the then newly-formed Farnham Society suggested that it should be left as it was. In the 1950s, the

NOS 49 & 51, ABBEY STREET, SHOWING ATTRACTIVE PAVING WITH BLUE BRICK PAVIORS.

Farnham Society placed a plaque on the building to mark the birth there in 1763 of William Cobbett, and the pub got its present name. The building is not recorded as an inn or alehouse until the mid-19th century, but there was a house called Teynter Acre on the site in the early 1700s.

But the biggest change in the famous view of Bridge Square did not happen. If the Maltings had been demolished in the 1960s, and replaced with maisonettes as proposed, things would have been very different. It seems inconceivable now that such a thing could have happened, but it so nearly did. The whole site was bought from Courages by the people of Farnham, including the 19th century Maltings and also the ancient Tanyard House and cottages in Red Lion Lane. The Maltings Association was set up, to become an independent arts and community centre. The houses were bought by the Farnham (Building Preservation) Trust and have gradually been restored and sold, Tanyard House in particular having been an award-winning project.

Bridge Square and its surroundings do indeed sum up many of Farnham's qualities; not just its history and evolution, but also the determination of its people not to see their inheritance lost.

RED LION LANE

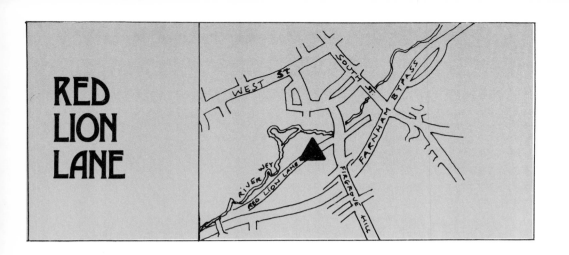

A gently curving, level village street, without pavements, lined with old cottages and low brick garden walls, with no traffic apart from some parked cars — this is Red Lion Lane which became a cul-de-sac when the missing central link in the Farnham Bypass was opened after the war. The road now runs from Bridge Square to come to an abrupt end at the side of the dual carriageway, except for the little spur of Weydon Mill Lane, leading to the river and the site of the long-gone mill.

On the south side of the road, cottages nestle up against the steep bank which shields them from the bypass and provides a picturesque backdrop, with dizzily sloping gardens and a fringe of trees. The road runs parallel to the river, and between houses on that side there are glimpses of Bishops Meadows, with the white tower and red-tiled roof of the church seen above a frieze of riverside willows.

There are no pubs in Red Lion Lane today, although as one would expect in a brewing town like Farnham, there were several at one time. The Red Lion Brewery was started by the Barrett family in the mid-19th century, on the site of the Maltings, and the Red Lion pub was to the left of the gates which lead into the courtyard. The Barratts lived in the house opposite now called The Old Malthouse, which was previously Old Roof and originally Elm Grove, neighbour to Fir Grove further up the hill. There is a network of tunnels and cellars under the hillside behind the house, probably once used as storage for barrels.

The brewery business was amalgamated later with Robert Sampson's maltings, which occupied the site slightly to the east, and the sign "Sampson Sampson Licensed Maltster" can still be seen painted on the wall of No. 8 Bridge Square.

Before the brewery, the western half of the Maltings site was a tannery, and Tanyard House, dating from 1500 and one of the oldest buildings in Farnham, must have been the home of a rich tanner because it was built on an unusually grand scale.

There used to be two other public houses or alehouses in Red Lion Lane — the Lion and Unicorn about halfway along, and the White Lion just beyond it.

Red Lion Lane today, with the river meadows alongside it and its traffic taken away by the bypass, is a pleasant and peaceful place.

Michael Blower Dec '87

RED LION LANE.

30   32   34   36

BUILDINGS IN SOUTH STREET, NOW DEMOLISHED.

M Blower.

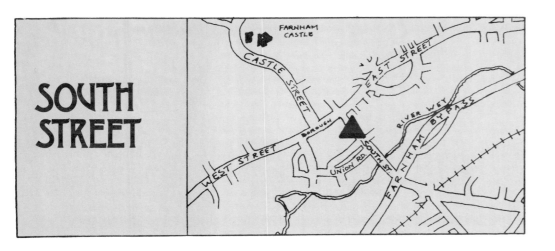

SOUTH STREET

This was South Street about the turn of the century, and in the first half of the century little changed, apart from the building in the 1930s of the Bush House terrace of shops and flats, and the neo-Georgian Royal Deer on the corner of East Street. The second half of this century, however, saw the disappearance of much of the street's Victorian character.

METHODIST CHURCH & MONTROSE HOUSE, SOUTH STREET.

South Street, with Union Road connecting it to Downing Street and Longbridge across what was once the town's cricket ground, is the newest of Farnham's central streets. It was built in the late 1860s to provide a direct route from the station to the town centre, following the opening of the railway 20 years earlier. It was at first known as New Road.

The new road was soon built up with solid Victorian and Edwardian buildings. On the corner of Abbey Street was the imposing three-storey brick building housing Hickley & Co., builders' merchants and suppliers of hardware. The area between the river bridge and the corner of Union Road, along the edge of Gostrey Meadow, was also built up, and further up on the west side of the road were the 'Surrey Iron' building, the Farnham School of Art, the Congregational church and the Farnham Institute, with the Bush Hotel and Ransom's the caterers (later Barclays Bank) at the junction with the Borough.

On the other side of the road, opposite Union Road, was the group consisting of the Farnham Council Offices, Montrose House, the Methodist Church, and the Lutyens Liberal Club, with the Farnham Auction Mart and some shops further up, on the edge of the cattle market.

SOUTH STREET IN 1979.

On the corner of Abbey Street, Hickley's buildings were knocked down in the 1970s, to make way for the widening of the main road. New buildings replaced the old ones near the river, and in the mid-1980s the buildings on the southern corner of the Union Road junction went too, to make room for a huge neo-classical office development which also absorbed and replaced an unloved 1960s building in Union Road — Expedier House. At the top of South Street, the old Barclays Bank building disappeared, and a bland post-modern edifice took its place.

The drawing of the view looking down South Street from the Borough end was done in the late 1970s, and it shows a street which still appears mainly Victorian in character, with substantial buildings which are two or three storeys in height and have an urban formality. The cattle market has become a car park, behind iron railings and two small bus shelters, and the building line is relieved by large trees.

BUILDINGS IN SOUTH STREET, NOW DEMOLISHED, DRAWN FROM THE
GARDEN OF THE UNITED REFORMED CHURCH.

69

BUILDINGS IN SOUTH STREET, DEMOLISHED TO MAKE WAY FOR SAINSBURYS SUPERMARKET

This view was substantially changed when Sainsbury's new supermarket was built at the beginning of the 1980s. A block of buildings on the east side of the road was demolished and replaced by a complex of retail, office, and delivery areas, with a 2-storey car park, all built on a very different scale. The new main building, of a featureless, barn-like design, was built at a right angle to the street instead of parallel to it as the older buildings had been, and the long walls of the car park were set back some distance from the road. The result is a street which now lacks form, integrity and style.

SAINSBURYS SUPERMARKET, OPENED IN 1983.

N Blower. Sept 1989.

A SUPERMARKET IN SOUTH STREET, AS HAROLD FALKNER MIGHT HAVE DESIGNED IT   Nov 16th 1979

There is a possibility, contained as a proposal in the 1984 Waverley Local Plan, that a new road will be built linking South Street with Dogflud Way. This would mean knocking down Montrose House to permit the road to emerge beside the council offices opposite the end of Union Road, and it would inevitably fragment the attractive group of which Montrose House is a part.

Some buildings in South Street have, however, been restored. The tall 'Surrey Iron' building on the corner of Union Road has been smartened up and now takes its place proudly in the perspective of the street.

SOUTH STREET IN 1988 - CORNER OF UNION ROAD WITH NEW BUILDINGS ON THE LEFT

M Blower,
Sept 88

73

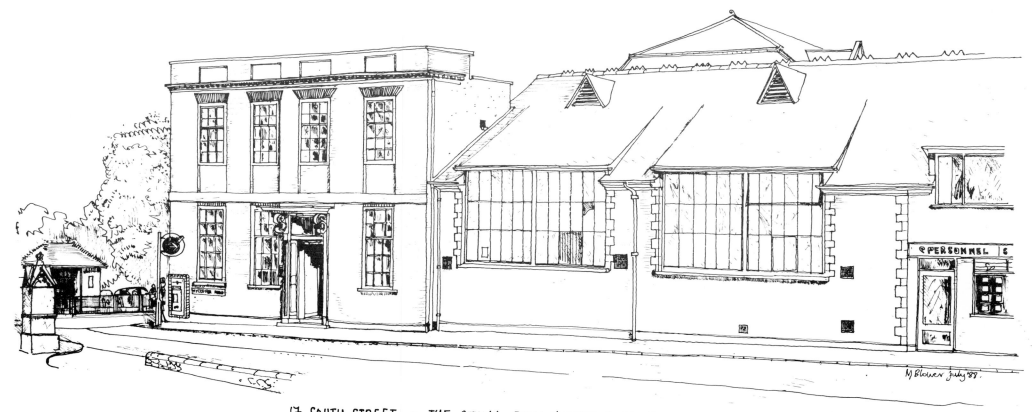

17. SOUTH STREET & THE STUDIO FROM VICTORIA ROAD IN 1988

17 South Street, the square 18th century block which was designed by Harold Falkner for the Farnham School of Art, was neglected in recent years after the Farnham Urban District Council Treasurer's Department moved out. This building was one of a series of premises occupied by the Farnham Art School, which began its life in the upper room of the Bailiff's Hall in the Borough, in 1865. It was established in South Street in the 1870s, with a studio behind in Victoria Road. W.H. Allen became its Head in 1889, and one of his earliest pupils, upon whom he had a profound influence, was the architect Harold Falkner, who designed the corner building in 1915. In 1939 the school moved to West Street, although the studio in Victoria Road was retained for some years, and it continued to grow in importance to become what it is now, the West Surrey College of Art and Design with its own 16-acre site in Falkner Road, at the top of the Hart.

17 South Street has been restored, and the studio behind it, with its high north lights, has been re-born in a neo-classical style to be used as offices in conjunction with the corner block. Few people remember now that it was the studio where Harold Falkner learned from his mentor W.H. Allen to value the design and craftsmanship of Georgian buildings, and that it was a small but significant part of the history of art in Farnham.

The Farnham Forge   Upper Church Lane.

Michael Blower 7 Sept 88

75

THE CHURCH LANES

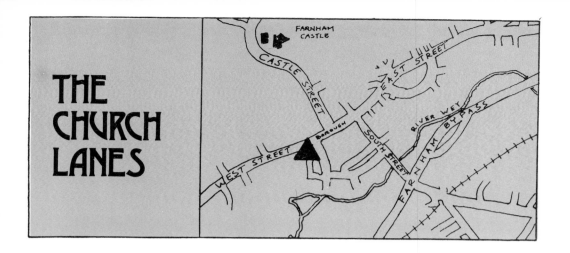

The view of Upper Church Lane from the churchyard gate presents an enchanting piece of streetscape. Here in the heart of Farnham's old centre, Upper, Middle and Lower Church Lane form three sides of a rectangle with Downing Street as the fourth, and this is one of the most picturesque parts of the town.

In the foreground of the drawing is the Farnham Forge, a long single-storey building filling in the space on the corner, between two taller houses. The forge is built of a mixture of brick and ironstone, its green-painted stable door decorated with samples of the blacksmith's art — long ornamental hinges ending in curlicues, a horseshoe for a doorknocker, and the word 'Blacksmith' on the flap of the letterbox. Six large stones held in place by iron rods, presumably mounting blocks, give the impression that they are supporting the building's slight forward lean.

The road narrows towards Downing Street, with whitewashed and red brick cottages close to the road leaving just enough space for a few bright flowers against their walls. On the other side of the lane is the high wall enclosing the garden of the rectory, which like so many Farnham walls is made of varied bricks of different shades, with even a patch of white chalkstone. A hawthorn tree leans over the wall.

This pleasant scene is set off by the most memorable feature of the Church Lanes, the historic surface of ironstone cobbles. These small narrow rectangular-shaped hard stones with a flat top cover the whole of the surface of Upper and Lower Church Lane, and most of Vicarage Lane. Middle Church Lane has been covered with tarmac, but there are cobbles at the side under the wall of the churchyard.

The stones are laid in a mosaic of different patterns. In the centre of the road, the stones are set at a right angle to the buildings, and in Lower Church Lane there is a drainage course down the middle marked by a line of larger rectangular stones edged with cobbles set parallel to the buildings. At the churchyard gate there is a broad triangle of stones set vertically, edged with longer stones laid end to end.

There is great art in the patterning of these cobblestones. Although they are not the most comfortable surface to walk on, they create beautiful textural contrasts, and they are genuinely old as opposed to the fake antiquity of the Lion and Lamb Yard cobbles. They have been poorly maintained in recent years, and deserve expert attention.

The drawing opposite shows Middle Church Lane, seen from the garden of The Rectory.

MIDDLE CHURCH LANE, FROM THE RECTORY GARDEN.

77

THE BOROUGH/ WEST STREET

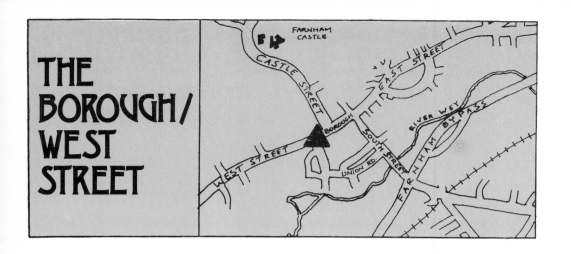

West Street and the Borough meet in the middle of the line of buildings shown in the drawing (opposite). No. 122 West Street is the tall Victorian-fronted building with projecting first-floor windows, for many years a wine merchants' but now a bookshop. No. 1 the Borough is Rumbelows, with its first floor timber framing.

Farnham street numbers have the unusual habit of running consecutively along one side of the road and then back along the other, instead of odds one side and evens the other. Thus No. 1 West Street is Alliance House on the corner of Downing Street, with No. 122 opposite.

At the top of Downing Street, where there is now a traffic island, was the site of the Round House, shown on old maps but demolished at the end of the 18th century when the road was widened to accommodate the demands of the growing coaching trade.

No. 121 West Street (Argos, previously the International Stores) and No. 122 (Hammicks Extra), although they look dissimilar, were originally one property on the site of the George Inn, which from the 16th century to the mid-18th century was a large and important hostelry. The remains of an old coaching

yard still survive behind the building, which was re-fronted in the 18th century. The property was divided in 1865 and the two parts now appear very different, as No. 122 was given a Victorian front with bay windows and an extra floor.

No. 1 the Borough is a curious mixture of styles which has been described as a Tudor sandwich. Its original front was cemented over in the 19th century, but in 1954 the underlying timber framing was exposed at first floor level. The archway on the right of the building leads to a small yard, from which it can be seen that the back of the building looks much older than the front — so often the case in Farnham.

The line continues with the long facade of Woolworths, which also has an opening leading to a yard, and then to a smaller building with a Venetian first floor window.

This interesting sequence of buildings, in the centre of Farnham, faces a focal point without a focus, a blank and featureless three-sectioned traffic island. The Round House cannot be reconstructed, and Farnham has no equivalent of the delightful Pepperpot building in Godalming. At the very least there ought to be a tree.

BUILDINGS AT THE MEETING POINT OF THE BOROUGH AND WEST STREET

THE BUSH HOTEL

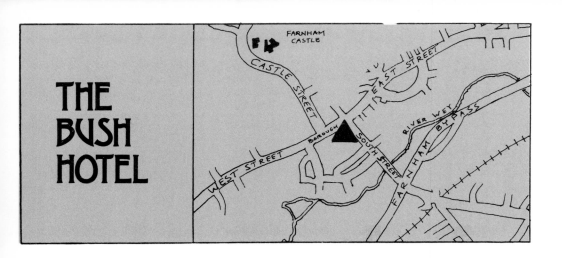

As he passed along West Street and the Borough it crossed his mind how, not so very long ago, his greatest treat had been to come in with Dick and old Barnaby to see the Farnham Horse Fair . . . Lights still lingered in many windows and from the celebrated 'Bush' Inn there came a cheerful glow and a sound of eager voices.

From To Right the Wrong
by Edna Lyall.

This tantalising snippet from a Victorian novel is quoted in an old brochure, painting a picture of the warmth and hospitality for which The Bush Hotel has a long tradition. Nobody seems to know for certain when it first opened its doors, but it is thought that there was an inn or alehouse on the spot in the 12th century, and 'The Bush' is one of the oldest inn names in the country, deriving from the bush of ivy, sacred to Bacchus, which was hung above the door of an inn from earliest times to indicate that wine was served there.

Farnham has always been a crossroads town, a place where you would expect to find a hostelry to welcome weary travellers. In Roman, Saxon and Norman times it was the meeting point of trackways used by traders, and the Pilgrims' Way, following the chalk ridges from Winchester to Canterbury, passed through the town.

Farnham Castle and Waverley Abbey, both built in the 12th century, would have attracted many visitors, and by the beginning of the 17th century when James I visited the Castle, The Bush was already described as "an ancient Inn". In 1618, the Judges of the Kings Bench declared it to be an inn and not just an alehouse; it was a rendezvous in the time of the Civil War, and Cromwell is believed to have stayed there in 1642.

In **The Virginians,** Thackeray wrote in 1857: "They reached the Bush at Farnham under which name a famous inn had stood in Farnham town for over three hundred years".

Some parts of the present building — notably the oldest brickwork, the oak beams, and the timber framed walls in the lounge — are 17th century. Frescoes painted on wood panelling in the lounge were done in about 1740, and it appears that the hotel was then being enlarged. An advertisement in the Daily

THE BUSH HOTEL, FROM THE BOROUGH.

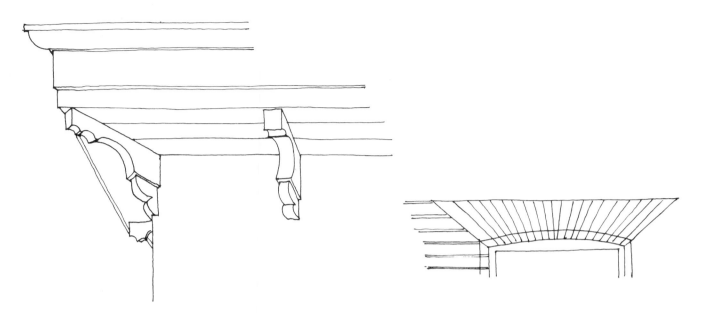

DETAIL OF CORNICE AND WINDOW, THE BUSH HOTEL.

Advertiser in 1742 announced: "This is to acquaint the publick that the Bush Inn in Farnham, Surrey is now opened and fitted up for the accommodation of gentlemen and others who may depend on being well accommodated".

Stage coaches called at The Bush for many years, clattering in from The Borough through the archway into the courtyard. It has long been a centre for local events, such as the Venison Feast begun by James I (which still continues, although it is now held at the Castle) and the 'Hop Betting Dinners' where local growers laid bets on the profitability of the year's crop.

In about 1840, the 18th century red-brick buildings were re-faced on the Borough front with yellow brick, and a hundred years later there were more changes when new shops were built along the road edge. The hotel then got its present 1930s-style splayed entrance, with shop windows curving back from the street line towards the courtyard, as the drawing shows. The back of the old brick archway is still visible from the courtyard, which nowadays is furnished with statues and a baroque fountain, and ornamental tables where people sit quietly sipping their drinks — all very different from the old days of stage coaches and highwaymen.

The entrance archway is floored, not with stone cobbles like the rest of the courtyard, but with worn wooden blocks extending in a strip to the centre — presumably to lessen the noise of early-morning coach wheels and reduce disturbance to sleeping customers.

Until the 1980s, the courtyard had a second opening leading through to South Street where the 19th century Bush Tap stood. This has now been closed off and has become the hotel's reception area, also reached from South Street. On this side of the building, a very unusual intricately ornamented chimney towers above the roof ridge — a chimney with a history, which was originally one of a pair on Norman Shaw's giant four-storey bank building at 75 Castle Street. When this building was demolished in the early 1930s, both chimneys were salvaged by Charles Borelli and Harold Falkner who were then working on the new Town Hall Buildings. One chimney was reinstated at the eastern end of the Town Hall Buildings, opposite the Bush in the Borough, and the other was placed at the Bush's South Street entrance.

In 1900, in a little town guide by Arthur Hart called **Farnham Past and Present,** The Bush is described as having grounds amounting to nearly three acres with gardens, a tennis lawn, and a bowling green. There was a large banqueting hall, and dining, drawing, billiard and private sitting rooms. A contemporary brochure offers a hotel for families and gentlemen, with "electric light, posting in all branches, motor cars on hire, garage with pit, and a bus meeting all trains."

Nowadays the grounds of the hotel have shrunk, although its buildings have grown with an extension at the side of the garden. The tennis court has become — predictably — a car park, but the garden is still a green oasis in the town centre traffic and the approach to the hotel from Victoria Road is its most attractive, up a paved path shaded with dark yew trees to a sunny terrace.

Here the old buildings are seen at their best, looking on to the sheltered garden with its lawn, rosebeds and small fish pond. The entrance door is shown in the drawing, under its impressive portico which shines white among the crowding leaves of the ivy covering the wall. With the heavy door standing wide open to display the arched passage and courtyard door opposite, the Bush Hotel welcomes its visitors now as it has done for hundreds of years, with the hospitality born of its long tradition.

GARDEN DOOR AT THE BUSH HOTEL.

PORTLAND HOUSE & PORTLAND TERRACE

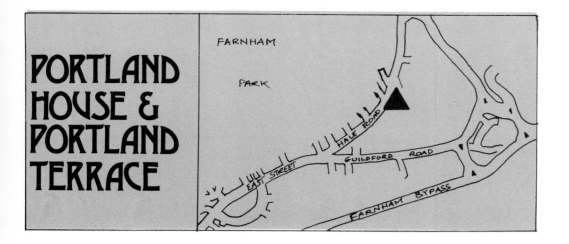

In 1989, Portland Terrace was still empty and a source of frustration to those who felt it was a wasted asset. The buildings are worth saving because they are part of a fast-diminishing stock of good Victorian building on the east side of Farnham, and because with their neighbour Portland House they form a group which is an important feature in Hale Road. Their restoration would be a worthwhile project.

The names of Portland House and Portland Terrace are probably unfamiliar to Farnham people, even if they pass the buildings on the edge of Farnham Hospital property in Hale Road every day. The drawing shows this Victorian group from the new development of Haven Way opposite, near Manor Road which leads from Hale Road into the hospital grounds. St Andrew's nurses' home, which used to stand beside them, was knocked down some years ago to make way for the hospital laundry building whose glistening silver chimney can be seen in the drawing.

Both Portland House, the substantial three-storey building, and 1-3 Portland Terrace, the cottages next to it, are the property of the local health authority. Portland House is used as staff accommodation by the hospital, and is well maintained. In contrast, the three cottages forming Portland Terrace have been empty since 1983, their doors boarded up and their tiny front gardens choked with weeds.

Repeated attempts by Waverley Council and other bodies to obtain a lease on the cottages so that they can be used to house homeless people have been frustrated by the possibility that a new ambulance station might be built on the site, but planning permission was refused in 1988.

PORTLAND HOUSE, DETAIL.

84

PORTLAND HOUSE & PORTLAND TERRACE, FROM HAVEN WAY

M. Blower. 6/88

85

BOUNDSTONE POST OFFICE.

OUT OF TOWN SHOPS ~ BOUNDSTONE

OUT OF TOWN SHOPS ~ RIDGWAY ROAD

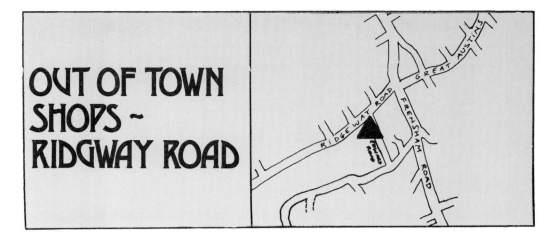

Town centres have got busier in recent years. In small towns like Farnham, streets are crowded, car parks are full, and food shopping has become dominated by supermarkets which vie with one another to offer a more and more ambitious service.

In this setting, a quick trip to a shop to pick up a loaf of bread or some fresh vegetables has become for many people an out-of-town activity instead of an in-town one. Small local corner shops have risen to the challenge and have become 'convenience stores' selling small quantities of just about everything, from a pound of potatoes to a packet of picture hooks.

There are many of these shops, sometimes with sub-Post Offices, all over the outlying parts of Farnham. Some stay open for up to 14 hours a day, 7 days a week; some specialise in locally-baked bread or locally-produced meat; and they are all small shops, selling a big range of goods, and offering a friendly local service. In these shops people still recognise one another, and they chat and pass the time of day. Their existence is a logical consequence of the mass-produced service offered in super-markets, and of the overcrowded town centres.

One such shop is Boundstone Post Office and Granger's Stores, in a lovely rural setting in Sandrock Hill Road, just past the lowest point of the dip where the road narrows almost to the width of a lane and begins to climb uphill again. The shop is in a small single-storey extension beside the road, attached to a neat

symmetrical house built of flint, with conspicuous bands of brick across it under a slate roof. This house, with its triangle of lawn in front and its straight garden path leading to two brick pillars at the gate, is the focal point of the view from the Wrecclesham end of Sandrock Hill Road. It sits in the centre of the picture, set against a dark background of oak trees, forming a charming country cameo.

The house appears, just as it is today, in a 19th century photograph published in Jean Parratt's **Bygone Farnham.** The surroundings have changed out of recognition, but the house is still the same.

In Ridgway Road there is a group of local shops, forming its own small centre. These shops occupy converted dwelling houses, their front gardens paved to form an attractive open space. The drawing shows the greengrocer's and florist's shop, with its striking iron balustrade, once painted a brilliant blue but now a sober black, above the first floor windows. Next to it is the general shop, in a double gabled house with a 'builder's trademark' which appears on other houses nearby, a design of bunches of grapes set above the windows. With a tree in front of it, the group of shops sits easily in its residential surroundings.

There are out-of-town shops like this all over the Farnham area, humming with activity and very much a part of the local community.

SHOPS IN RIDGWAY ROAD.

THE WELLINGTON, HEATH END.

89

THE WELLINGTON

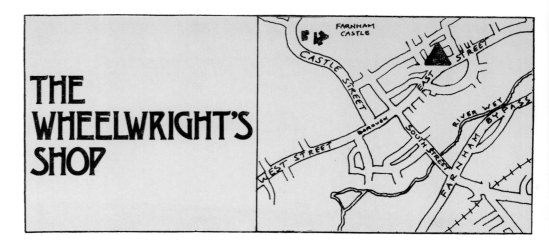

The building which for many years was the Wellington public house is a familiar landmark in the Farnborough Road, in its position beside the traffic lights at the Alma Lane junction. Its corner site, and upstanding square facade fronting the main road, make it very noticeable beside its neighbouring terrace of small slate-roofed cottages.

The Wellington is mainly built of the rounded flint stones which are characteristic of Heath End and Hale, and which can still be found on the local heath land. In this part of Farnham bricks were used sparingly in 19th century buildings, and in the Wellington the flints provide the principal material of the wall construction, held in by brick dressings at the outer corners and around the windows. On the road front, the facade has been raised above eaves level so that it stands out in the perspective view, with a broad white band running across it carrying the name 'The Wellington' in relief lettering.

The Wellington and the cottages next door to it were built about 1860, after the army came to Aldershot and part of the surge of local development which followed that event. Needless to say, pubs were in demand by the soldiers who came to spend their off duty time in Farnham, and the Wellington was one of several built at this time.

In recent years the pub became an off-licence, and the drawing shows the building as it was in the middle of 1988 when the business had just closed down, and it was up for sale. A sub-Post Office in the cottage next door had also closed. In 1989 the Wellington became a kitchen design shop — perhaps an indication of changing priorities in the 1980s?

THE WHEELWRIGHT'S SHOP

The wheelwright's shop in East Street, on the corner of St Cross Road, was made famous by George Sturt in his book written at the turn of the century under the name George Bourne. The author described the shop belonging to his grandfather, also called George Sturt, who had worked for William Grover, a wheelwright who started a shop on the site in 1795. In fact the link goes back even further, to George Draper who bought part of a hopground in 1706 and began the association of the site with the wheelwright's trade.

It was probably William Grover who built the shop and houses next to it in East Street which were later owned by the Sturt family. The shop passed to George Sturt the author through his father, and at the turn of the century it had become Sturt and

THE WHEELWRIGHT'S SHOP IN 1987.

Goatcher, coachbuilders, which was taken over by Arnold and Comben in 1920.

The old wheelwright's shop on the corner, with the cottages next to it, remained until the late 1980s, although the front of the shop was obscured by a flat roofed mainly glass fronted 1920s extension with heavy Doric columns and a stucco plinth. The premises were occupied by a motor bike shop, as shown in the drawing.

Behind the cottages there had been a chapel built by the Independent Congregation of Dissenters in about 1792, with a burial ground in front of it. Next to it was the British School, built in 1833 for the children of non-conformists, which, until its conversion into a motor showroom in 1960 was said to be of an architectural quality comparable with houses in West Street.

In 1988 the whole of this large site was taken over by Swain & Jones, and in the summer of 1989 it was opened as a new showroom for Jaguar cars, with the wheelwright's shop reconstructed and containing a small museum recording its famous past. It is nice to reflect that in this way, the long tradition of wheels going back nearly 300 years has been preserved.

CASTLE STREET

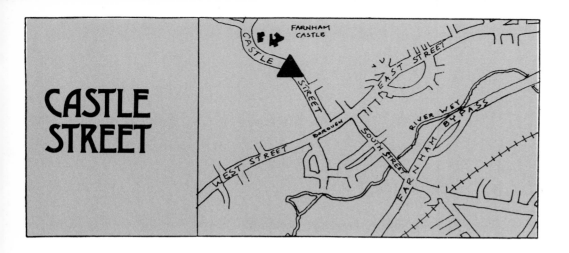

There are two famous views of Castle Street. From the bottom of the hill in The Borough, the vista stretches upward, stately buildings lining each side of the wide street as it climbs to meet the thick band of trees which partly hide the Castle. Coming down the hill, the panorama of the street opens up with breathtaking suddenness around a bend in a broad sweep of Georgian elegance ending in the commanding square block of the 19th century National Westminster Bank.

These are the well-known views of a much-praised piece of streetscape, presenting a scene of classic grace and beauty. But in fact Farnham's Georgian style is only skin-deep; it was superimposed on an unpretentious working town which had always done well, but which became especially successful in the 18th century, and got smartened up. The pre-Georgian character of an older, simpler Farnham is still there despite appearances, just below the surface.

We have therefore chosen to end this book with a view which shows some of the less obvious qualities of Castle Street, the small-scale, homely side of its character. The drawing was done from the end of the narrow passageway on the west side of the street which leads to Lowndes Buildings. Two houses on the opposite side of the street are framed by high walls, caught in a snapshot view with a lamp-post posing in front of them.

This lamp-post is one of nineteen in Castle Street which were individually listed in the early 1970s to protect them from the wholesale replacement of old lamps which was taking place at the time. This is No. 15, tall, with rather severe lines, and a fluted standard which is heavy at the base and tapering to a slender proportion at the top, where small curved brackets support the handsome glass lamp. These lamps have now become an inseparable part of Castle Street's image, and it would indeed have been sad if they had been lost.

The tiny passageway from which the drawing was done slips unobtrusively away from the main street through a gap between two houses, to open up at the attractive terrace of Lowndes Buildings, a row of cottages with bright front gardens edged with iron railings. The footpath goes on to connect with Long Garden Walk in the community of small houses and industries which lie hidden there behind Castle Street's outward face, a quiet area with old stables and storage buildings which grew up to serve the bigger houses and businesses in the street.

The two houses in the drawing are Nos. 46 and 47 Castle Street, a little above the Windsor Almshouses with their towering plane trees, and the Nelson Arms public house. They are just at the point where front gardens begin, so that No.46, higher up the hill, has a pretty garden with flowers and clumps of blue lavender behind railings, and No. 47 has its doors on the edge of the pavement. Both houses are simple in style, although the facade of No. 46 has been raised and parapeted to give it a more formal appearance. They are built of warm red Farnham brick with welcoming white painted windows under tiled roofs whose ridge line dips under the weight of centuries.

These two little houses, with the lamp-post in front of them, framed by the enclosing walls of the passageway, represent Castle Street's less obvious qualities. It is not just a picture postcard, it is a place where people live and work, the beating heart of a real town. To Farnham people it is as it has been for centuries, their home.

MBGowen. 6/89